AF339301

GOING THE DISTANCE

GOING
THE
DISTANCE

A Manual of
Long Distance Riding

Sue Parslow

DAVID & CHARLES
Newton Abbot · London

David & Charles Equestrian Titles

BEHAVIOUR PROBLEMS IN HORSES
Susan McBane
BREEDING AND TRAINING A HORSE OR PONY
Ann Sutcliffe
CHAMPION HORSES AND PONIES
Pamela Macgregor-Morris
COMPLEAT HORSE
Johannes E. Flade
DRESSAGE Begin the Right Way
Lockie Richards
EQUINE FITNESS
Dr David Snow and Colin Vogel
GYMKHANA!
Lesley Eccles and Linda Burgess
THE HEAVY HORSE MANUAL
Nick Rayner and Keith Chivers
THE HORSE AND THE LAW
Donald Cassell
HORSE BREEDING
Peter Rossdale
HORSE DRIVING TRIALS The Art of Competitive Coachmanship
Tom Coombs
THE HORSE'S HEALTH FROM A TO Z An Equine Veterinary Directory
Peter Rossdale and Susan M. Wreford
THE HORSE OWNER'S HANDBOOK
Monty Mortimer
THE HORSE RIDER'S HANDBOOK
Monty Mortimer
HUNTING An Introductory Handbook
R.W.F. Poole
THE IMPERIAL HORSE The Saga of the Lipizzaners
Hans-Heinrich Isenbart and Emil Buhrer
KEEPING A HORSE OUTDOORS
Susan McBane
LUNGEING The Horse and Rider
Sheila Inderwick
THE RIDING INSTRUCTOR'S HANDBOOK
Monty Mortimer
RIDING AND STABLE SAFETY
Ann Brock
TRANSPORTING YOUR HORSE OR PONY
Chris Larter and Tony Jackson

Contents

TO PRIMA

ACKNOWLEDGEMENTS
The author wishes to thank the following:
Maggie Moreton, BHS Long Distance Riding Group; Dr Reidler, ELDRIC;
Pam James; Rod Fisher; Hadyn Price; the Arab Horse Society; David Snow;
Jane Welcher; Sue Broughton; Joan Davies; Rosemary Attfield; Douglas
Whitehead; Roger Hatch of Bartholomews; Jan Field-Byrne; Jill Thomas;
Margaret Montgomerie and Margaret Swords, and many other BHS and EHPS
members who have been kind enough to pass on information about their sport
and their horses. Also, thanks to Adrian Colston and my father for allowing me
to use their word processors. Special thanks to Lesley Eccles for giving me the
opportunity to write this book, and to my husband Jon for putting up with
me while I wrote it!

British Library Cataloguing in Publication Data
Parslow, Sue
   Going the distance: a manual of long
   distance riding.
   1. Livestock: Horses. Endurance riding–
   Manuals
   I.Title
   798.2'3
ISBN 0-7153-9150-X

Typeset by Typesetters (Birmingham) Ltd,
Smethwick, Warley, West Midlands
and printed in Great Britain
by Butler & Tanner Limited, Frome and London
for David & Charles Publishers plc
Brunel House Newton Abbot Devon

1 The Organisation of the Sport

DISTANCE RIDING EXPLAINED

Long distance and endurance riding offers a unique and special challenge for the horse and rider as the horse must cover many miles of varied terrain and still arrive at the finish fit and sound.

Very simply, the idea behind long distance riding is for the horse to be ridden over a set distance at a set speed, both dictated by the level of competition. The fitness and condition of the horse is judged by veterinary inspections at the start and finish of the ride, and in the middle of longer rides. If the horse fails these checks on any point, then the combination will be eliminated; this ensures that the horse is never in any danger of injuring himself.

In preparing for a long distance ride the rider develops an affinity with the horse by constantly monitoring his health and state of fitness. A special bond grows between the two and when the ultimate effort is demanded they become a source of encouragement and support to one another; they must trust each other.

The rider must be able to detect how well the horse is performing and coping with the terrain and must adjust the pace and riding technique accordingly, perhaps even accepting a lower award to save asking too much of the horse.

Many uninformed people imagine that this sport is a soft option, an extension of going for a lazy Sunday hack. Well, sometimes long distance riding does attract riders who ask nothing more than to enjoy the countryside on horseback. But this is not what endurance riding is all about. It is a serious sport requiring many hours of training and preparation. There are often long distances to travel to competitions as you become more involved. Many people like to explore new areas, and rides are held in some of the most scenic areas of the country.

While no special skills are required, both horse and rider need to be fit enough to cope with the chosen level of competition. Good stable management is required – feeding a fit horse correctly is a skill in itself, and the higher you go the more accomplished you must become.

One of the great things about long distance riding is the feeling of comradeship – the newcomer may often find himself riding alongside a 'seasoned campaigner' or perhaps a European champion and will be treated as an equal. The atmosphere at competitions is relaxed and infor-mal, mainly because a rider can set a personal goal in achieving a certain award time on distance. On endurance rides the element of 'competition'

(page 7) The majority of competitive rides are based on bridleways and byways
(Steve Moore)

comes only at the end when riders may race for first position. What appeals to many people about the sport is that they are always making new discoveries about their horse and his natural abilities; on each ride they may have to ask something different and can gauge his response.

An ambition of many riders is to complete a 100 mile (160km*) ride. This is within the grasp of many, though it may take three years of preparation and competition to achieve.

RIDES AVAILABLE

Long distance rides are graded so that the newcomer can start at the bottom without fear of either over-taxing his horse or himself, and progress gradually up the scale. It can take two or three years to have the horse ready to compete over 100 miles.

· PLEASURE RIDES ·

These are non-competitive rides designed to be an introduction to long distance riding. Any horse and rider can take part without necessarily having to be a member of the organising group. The rides cover distances of between 10 and 25 miles – most are over 20 miles. Usually, a minimum speed of 5mph (8km) is given – that of an average hack – just to make sure particpants don't dawdle.

Most pleasure rides start at the same venue as higher grade rides and follow the same route for a while before looping back, although in Britain the BHS LDRG and EHPS fixture lists do include pleasure rides which are organised separately. The BHS also runs training rides, often in conjunction with other ride classes, where the leader will offer guidance along the ride. They can be at fast, medium or slow speeds, run between 5 and 10mph.

The EHPS has a countrywide network of local groups, usually one per about two counties, who give a warm welcome to newcomers and who regularly organise social and training rides and demonstrations. More and more riding clubs are arranging long distance rides for their members, usually on a sponsorship basis, and involve distances of 15, 20, or 25 miles. So there is no excuse of not having any rides to go to!

The great thing about pleasure rides is that you can cross some fabulous countryside and get a taste of what long distance riding is all about. On those rides which coincide with other classes you may rub shoulders with the country's best riders and perhaps pick up some useful tips. After this you may be eager to try out a competitive ride. These take

*Where mileage is not given in kilometres multiply the number of miles by 1.6.

different routes at this stage, depending on the organising body, whether BHS LDRG or EHPS.

EHPS

The EHPS runs Novice Rides, Competitive Trail Rides (CTRs), and Endurance Rides (ERs).

· NOVICE RIDES ·

These rides are between 20 and 25 miles (32 and 40km), run at a speed of 6 to 7 mph and are judged on the same basis as Competitive Trail Rides. Horses aged 5 years and upwards, which have not previously competed in EHPS events and are not graded, are eligible.

· COMPETITIVE TRAIL RIDES ·

CTRs have rides from 25 to 60 miles (40 to 96km). There are Novice, Junior and Open sections, the categories applying to the horses not the riders.

In the Novice section the horse or pony must be aged four or over – four-year-olds may take part but are not eligible for trophy or grading points. A five-year-old may be ridden in as many novice rides as the rider desires, but must upgrade to the Open section at the end of the season when it is awarded a grading.

The Junior section is open to horses or ponies aged 5 years and over, and riders 8 to 17 years. Under 12's must be accompanied by an adult en route at all times; under 10's are allowed at the discretion of the ride organiser and are permitted to ride a maximum of 30 miles (48km)

In the Open section horses must be 5 years and over, and riders over 18 on January 1. However, juniors aged 15 and over may upgrade to Senior Open.

At CTR level success is judged upon speed and the condition of the horse during and after the ride. For Open rides of 25 to 60 miles (40 to 96km) a speed of between 7 and 8mph is required and penalty points are given to speeds slower and faster than that; disqualification for extremes. Time penalties may also be incurred at the rate of one point for every three minutes or part of three minutes, exceeding the optimum time.

EHPS schedules also include Fast CTRs, which require a speed of between 8 and 9mph – the same rules for penalty points and elimination apply. These rides are ideal for experienced horses.

Veterinary judging plays a very important part in CTRs. Penalty points can be given on a sliding scale for pulse and respiration rates but if either or both are too high the horse will be eliminated.

Long-distance riding is a sport for all, from children to the retired, from small ponies to hunter-types (Steve Moore)

Similarly, penalties can be incurred for injuries and the horse will be eliminated if lame.

· ENDURANCE RIDES ·

Endurance rides are ridden at a faster pace and are actually races, over a minimum of 50 miles (80km) with a maximum of 100 miles (160.9km) in a day. To qualify for an ER the horse and rider must have been graded in at least two CTRs of 40 miles (64km), or have a combination of BHS bronze, silver, or gold awards.

There is a massed start and a minimum average speed. The first horse across the finish line who also successfully passes the veterinary inspection, is the winner. If two or more riders finish at the same time, then the 'tie-breaker' is the horse's pulse and respiration rates taken 30 minutes after the finish.

Each horse is checked over by a vet and has its pulse taken prior to the start, and during the ride there are mandatory halts and spot checks. The first of the latter may be about 4 or 5 miles after the start; the pulse rate is taken and if found to be above 64

A small group returning to the competition venue after completing a Bronze Buckle ride (Steve Moore)

the rider could be eliminated or held back until it has gone down, and the horse recovered.

The first halt on a 50 mile (80km) endurance ride is at the 25 mile (40km) mark lasting for half an hour, followed by a spot check at approximately 40 miles (64km). On a 100 mile (160km) ride there is a halt at 25 miles (40km), at 50 (80km) and at 75 (120km), with a spot check between 85 (136km) and 90 miles (144km). The horse must always be judged fit to continue.

Halts are controlled by gates, some with a timed hold. A sensible rider will plan for the halts in his ride tactics and cover the last mile or so in walk; his horse should then have low pulse rates and will therefore waste little time at the hold.

On arrival at the gate the competitor is given a card with his number on, together with the checkpoint number and his time of arrival. In the next twenty minutes the horse must be presented to the vet, who will assess the horse according to the parameters set for that gate – these vary according to the venue, site of the gate hold and the weather.

If the horse passes, the vet will immediately carry out the 60/60 (minute test), in which it must be trotted up for 30 metres and back again. This is timed by a stop watch for 60 seconds and the pulse is taken again, starting as soon as the stop watch reaches the 60 second mark. Any horse whose pulse is too high will be eliminated. The ride time restarts as soon as the minute test is completed. The appropriate times and parameters will be recorded on the rider's competitor card which must then be handed to the time-keeper on the way out. Each gate has a separate card.

If initially the horse fails it may be re-presented but not less than ten minutes after the first presentation. You really do have to watch your time here because if you are not careful your twenty minute total time will have run out.

As with CTRs there are separate divisions, according to the horse and rider's experience. For Senior Open and Junior, the competing horses must be over 6 for 75 mile rides, and over 7 for 100 mile rides.

In the Junior division the rider must be over 12 but less than 18, and up to 15 years, riders must be accompanied by an adult throughout the ride. In a 100 mile (160km) ride a doctor will examine the young riders during the second halt to decide if they are fit to continue.

At the time of writing the only 100 mile endurance ride in the EHPS calendar is the Summer Solstice ride, staged each year on the weekend nearest to the longest day. To qualify, horse and rider must have proof of having completed two 40 mile (64km) rides, CTR or ER, or a BHS LDRG·Golden Horseshoe qualifier, and a 50 mile ride – CTR, or Golden Horseshoe qualifier with a minimum speed of 7mph.

BHS
· BRONZE BUCKLE RIDES ·

This is the first in the three categories of ride organised by the BHS Long Distance Riding Group, and has two sections: Bronze Buckle qualifiers

The silver stirrup and bronze buckle, awards to be won on BHS Long Distance Ride Group rides (EMAP)

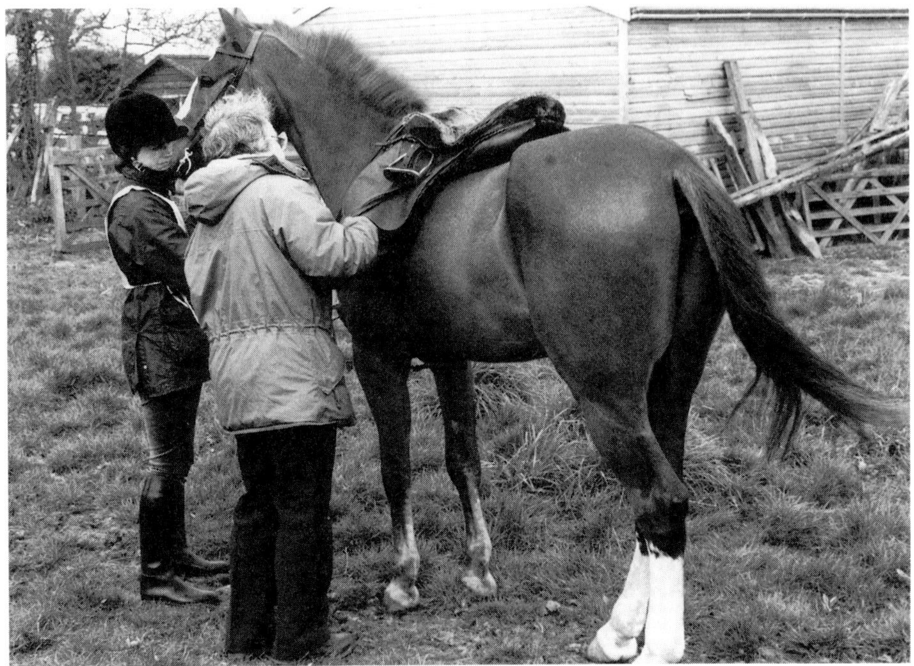

A BHS steward conducts a tack inspection at the start of a ride (Steve Moore)

and Bronze Buckle finals. The Qualifier is ridden over 20 miles (32km) at a minimum speed of $6^1/_2$ mph, and the Final over 30 miles at a speed of 7mph. The rider needs to compete successfully in only one Bronze Buckle qualifier to go on to a Bronze Buckle final. And the reward for successfully completing the latter really is a bronze buckle!

These rides are very popular and are an ideal progression from the pleasure ride; they are also valuable for attracting riders to the sport, since you don't even need to be a member of the BHS to take part.

Horses must be 4 years old and over, and young riders aged 10; up to 14 they are classed as Juniors and must be accompanied by an adult. Horses and ponies are vetted before and after the ride in the same way as in EHPS rides: a horse with a pulse rate of over 64, or exceeding the rate set on the day, will be eliminated.

· SILVER STIRRUP ·

Again, this category is divided into two: the Qualifier is ridden over 40 miles at 7mph, and the Final over 50 miles at $7^1/_2$ mph. Rewards for successful completion of the Qualifier are a rosette and certificate, and for the Final a rosette and miniature silver stirrup.

To take part at this level the rider must be a member of the British Horse Society, and the horse or pony must be over five years old and

BHS registered. The rider must also have a helper to ensure that the horse receives all the care and attention it needs. However, a Gold series rider (who has competed at Golden Horseshoe level) is not required to have a helper. Young riders must be at least 14 and be accompanied for the Qualifier, and be 15 plus for the Final in which they may be unaccompanied.

BHS long distance riders accumulate points to gain awards: one point per mile is awarded for the Bronze Buckle Finals or Silver Stirrup Qualifiers; two points per mile for completing the Silver Stirrup final and Gold qualifying rides; finally, three points per mile for all Gold series rides. Points can also be gained for completing one day of a two- or three-day ride, providing the horse passes the veterinary inspection at the end of the day.

· *GOLDEN HORSESHOE QUALIFIER* ·

Golden Horseshoe Qualifiers are ridden over 40 miles (64km) at $7^{1}/_{2}$ mph, and are held in the first half of the season leading up to the Golden Horseshoe ride in May. To take part, the rider must have completed the bronze and silver series rides, or have had the equivalent experience with the EHPS or Highland Long Distance Riding Club. Horses must be more than 6 years old.

· *GOLDEN HORSESHOE* ·

This is perhaps the best known of Britain's rides and is certainly the longest established. It covers approximately 100 miles (160km) over Exmoor's National Park and is divided 50/50 over two days. To take part in this major ride entrants must have successfully completed a Golden Horseshoe Qualifier in the same season.

The terrain over Exmoor is as varied as the weather and the route is changed every year, offering new challenges to horse and rider: stony tracks, springy turf, open moorland and wooded coombes, sharp ascents and steep descents. The weather can also present problems such as snow, fog or even extreme heat.

Awards are presented according to the veterinary penalties and speeds achieved. A Gold Award, a gold medal, is given to the combination which finishes with an average speed of 8mph or more on each day with no penalties. Silver and Bronze Awards, and rosettes, are presented on a sliding scale, according to lower speeds and the number of penalties (maximum number allowed for an award is 6).

N.B. Rules for rides may change so for full, up-to-date information please check the appropriate society's rule book.

2 History and Development

EARLY DAYS

It is hard to determine when long distance riding became a sport in its own right. What is certain is that without the horse the history of the human race would have been quite different. There would have been little travel across the continents, many battles would not have been fought nor territories conquered. Until the invention of the motor vehicle – which also owes something to the horse since the capacity of the engine is termed in horse power – our lives would have been restricted to the areas we were born in. There would have been no postal service and early industrial development would have been seriously limited.

Long distance riding must have the earliest origins of any equestrian sport. The first person to dare to climb onto a horse's back was no doubt bolted with for miles (if he'd managed to cling on!), but this experience probably gave him the idea of the horse as his transport and aid in hunting, rather than as the next meal. But unlike the dog who was probably man's companion long before the horse, the latter was far more spirited and took much more taming before it could be useful. But it is this very spirit and courage which lends itself to long distance riding. The horses that do well over the longer distance rides are those with that special something which will keep them going when the 'going' gets tough.

Ancient civilisations used the horse in their cavalries and must have ridden many thousands of miles, enduring harsh climates, hunger and fatigue. The Bedouin made some extraordinary journeys – one of the most exceptional was that of Si-ben-Zyam, who was ordered by his father to take his mare from Algiers to prevent her from being requisitioned by the Turks. He rode through the night, resting for only one hour and with just one stop to allow her to drink, and completed the distance of 240 miles in just 24 hours.

The Persians developed the first comprehensive system of communications, again thanks to horses: posting stations were placed one day's ride apart so that a 1,500 mile journey was covered using relays of horses, in 7 to 14 days. Eighteen hundred years later a similar system was used by Ghengis Khan whose riders rode approximately 150 miles a day.

The legendary Pony Express was created in 1860: mail was carried between Missouri and San Francisco by a series of riders who took it in relays through what was often hostile Indian territory – this was a total distance of 1,966 miles through Missouri, Kansas, Nebraska, Colorado, Wyoming, Utah, and Nevada to Sacramento, California. At one time the

(left)Alice Uttley and her Arab mare Sheba on one of the season's early rides
(Steve Moore)

Pony Express had 100 riders, 190 relay stations, 400 station staff and used an incredible 400 ponies in ten days. The fastest run was made over 120 miles (193km) in 8 hours 10 mins. Unfortunately, the Pony Express only lasted two years because of the losses it incurred.

In more recent times all sorts of horses have been ridden, led or worked across long distances. In the north of England for example, long 'trains' of pack horses carried wool from the Dales farms to the coastal ports of west Cumberland, returning with food, brandy, rum and tobacco, coping with long journeys over steep and hilly terrain. Barge horses had to walk for long distances each day, able to pull a 50–60 tonne load and keep it moving, but light and agile enough to clear any obstacles in their path.

Cavalries used horses to cover great distances. In one exercise in the 1930s, the horses had to complete a 90-mile endurance ride out of Cairo and back – they made the outward journey in three days, had a 24-hour break, and then returned in 12 hours without any injury or suffering to the horses.

Long distance riding as a sport probably began at the beginning of the century on the continent. Some tough race rides were run but these had disastrous results, with horses dying of exhaustion. One such race was run by the Prussian and Austro-Hungarian cavalries in 1892 from Berlin to Vienna, a distance of about 400 miles (643km). The race was won in 71 hours 27 mins and apart from 11 hours rest, the whole time was spent riding. By the end of the following week 25 horses had died, including the winner. In 1903 two horses died in a French ride, a two-day affair over a total distance of 133 miles (215km).

Rides like this gave long distance a bad name and a reputation which it has taken some time to shake off.

UNITED KINGDOM

The first long distance rides in Britain were run in the 1920s by the newly formed Arab Horse Society as endurance races, to demonstrate the Arab's stamina and persuade the War Office to introduce Arab blood into their cavalry mounts. Each horse carried 82.5kg (182lb [13 stone]) and covered a total distance of 300 miles in five days, with careful veterinary inspections before and after each day's ride. The first rides were held on the South Downs, starting near Lewes in Sussex, and ran for three consecutive years – this was the only time that tests of such length were held in Britain.

Today's sport began with a 'summer holiday on horseback' organised in 1937 by *Country Life* and *Riding* magazines. The finish was in

Eastbourne and competitors could choose any route so long as it was 100 miles (160km); a maximum of 30 miles (48km) was ridden in a day with regular checkpoints and veterinary examinations. This ride took place again two years later, but World War II cut short its career.

There were no long distance rides to speak of in Britain between the 'summer holiday' ride of 1939, and 1965 when the first Golden Horseshoe ride was held. The Arab Horse Society did organise a 225 mile (360km) ride, but it attracted only a few starters and none of them finished. In the same year that the BHS ran their first Golden Horseshoe, the AHS organised a 50 mile (80km) ride as a two-day trial at Goodwood, in which competitors rode 50 miles on the first day and took part in a Prix Caprilli test on the second.

· GOLDEN HORSESHOE ·

The AHS joined with the BHS three years later to run this 75 mile (120km) Golden Horseshoe ride. It remained a joint effort until 1975 when the BHS formed its Long Distance Riding Group and took full charge of the ride organisation.

The Golden Horseshoe has been held all over the country, over varying distances and with varying speeds. In 1974 it moved to Exmoor, and two years later the total distance was increased to 100 miles (160km) over two days, since many riders were proving that 75 miles, and gold awards, were well within their grasp and a new challenge was needed. At the same time a separate 50 mile ride was created. Held annually in May, the Golden Horseshoe has become Britain's prestige ride and one which many up-and-coming riders set as their goal.

Horses and riders must qualify for the ride by competing in a series of 40 mile rides held countrywide throughout the spring at BHS LDRG rides. In 1988 there were 14 of these rides between the beginning of March and the end of April. Horses must be at least 6 years old.

On the Golden Horseshoe Ride gold medals are awarded for completing the distance at 8mph, and silver and bronze medals, plus rosettes according to penalties incurred with varying speeds.

In 1973 a small group of enthusiasts formed the Endurance Horse and Pony Society (EHPS), now the largest long distance riding society in the UK. Their main objective was to promote the welfare of the horse in the sport. Two years after its formation the society organised the first 100 mile (160km) endurance ride ever run in Britain – the Summer Solstice. It was repeated two years later, though not in the summer so it could not keep the name. In its early years it was held on the South Downs, then moved to Sherwood Forest in Nottinghamshire where it has been staged in recent years in May. In 1988 it was held in Hexham, Northumberland.

The Summer Solstice is an endurance race run in one day and is the toughest and most competitive ride in the British long distance calendar. The placings are decided on time, provided that the horse passes the veterinary inspections fit and sound. It is now one of three international events run by the EHPS. The others are Breamore in Hampshire, a 50 mile (80km) endurance ride, and the Red Dragon in Wales, a two-day ride with 50 miles on each day.

The two organisations work side by side, recognising each other's qualifying rides, and most competitors belong to both and work out their own calendars from both fixture lists. In particular the two work together when selecting teams to compete abroad in championships.

· SCOTLAND ·

The vast highlands and lowlands of Scotland have a great deal to offer the long distance rider. Horses can be got fit very quickly and there is some wonderful scenery to explore.

The Highland Long Distance Riding Club has a thriving and enthusiastic membership of around 200. The group was formed in Inverness in 1982 and has numerous branches, each one organising its rides independently under HLDRC rules, but they may set their own entry fees; rosettes are awarded for mileage.

A wide variety of rides is offered, from pleasure rides of 10 miles (16km) to competitive classes up to 100 miles (160km) over two days. Riders and mounts tackle varied terrain which often provides spectacular views, though weather conditions can change as suddenly as the scenery.

The Scottish Championship is run over 100 miles (160km) in two days, and the venue changes each year – the club is always looking for challenging terrain. It has been held in the Loch Ness area and in 1988 it was held in Invarary, Argyll. It is the only race ride organised by HLDRC, and to qualify the combination must have successfully competed in the following: 100 miles (160km) over two days, 50 miles (80km) in one day, 40 miles (64km) over two days at 6mph (9km) and 40 miles (64km) over one day at 6mph (9km). Qualifications from other societies are accepted.

At the championship venue there are 50 (80km), 25 (40km) and 15 mile (24km) pleasure rides; riders have the choice of different speed categories, with best condition, bronze, silver and gold awards in each class. There is usually an annual Golden Horseshoe Qualifier in Scotland and a few riders make the long trek down to Exmoor to compete in the 100 mile (160km) final. However, it is quicker for most of the riders to travel to Scandinavia!

Organised charity rides are a tradition in Scotland. In 1986 a ride from Inverness to Ingliston raised over £2,000 for cancer research; it was approximately 170 miles (272km), took 6 days and was completed by six riders and six horses. The following year HLDRC organised a relay around Loch Ness.

The riders are renowned for being friendly – their motto is 'Come on – take up the Highland Challenge'; in fact, you don't have to be a member of the club to take part in any of their rides.

· *EAST ANGLIA* ·

The East Anglian Trail Riders' Association was formed by Dorothy 'Twiggy' Holmes of Dereham in Norfolk in 1975. It came about because she kept meeting riders who asked her where they could ride in the Norfolk/Suffolk area. Taking the initiative, she called a meeting in a pub one evening and was astounded when 27 people turned up. They were all keen to start up a group which would organise long distance rides and social activities.

At first they organised a range of unambitious events, the longest distance ride being 20 miles (32km). Many members were quite content with that and enjoyed riding in new surroundings in a 'social' atmosphere. Now, there are members who have gone on to greater things, including David Abercombie who was BHS National Points Champion in 1988. Quite a few compete in 100 mile rides, so the Association is a good 'launching pad'.

Membership of EATRA varies between 100 and 200. Rides and events take place throughout East Anglia, and organisers aim to have one ride a month at least. Details are listed in a twice yearly newsletter. The minimum ride distance is 10 miles (16km), and 30 miles (48km) the maximum. Most prefer the shorter distance since they can take part without having to spend a great deal of time training their horses.

EATRA is affiliated to the British Horse Society and so its ride calendar may include Bronze Buckle rides. Rides are run over scenic and interesting areas, for example Peddars Way, and the North Norfolk coast. There is a points system, the winner of which is awarded the Endeavour Trophy.

USA

America's famous Tevis Cup ride was first held in 1955 and has been organised annually in California ever since.

On 7 August 1955 the Sacramento Sheriff's posse, five riders led by Wendell Robie and Nick Mansfield, resolved to prove that modern riders had not gone soft and set out to emulate the achievements of the Pony Express riders. They followed the Old Emigrant trail over the Sierras from the Squaw Valley near Tahoe City, Nevada, along the Eldorado river 100 miles (160km) to Auburn, just short of Sacramento, California – it took 22 hours 25 mins and is now generally accepted as the toughest endurance ride in the world.

Competitors today ride 100 miles (160km) in 24 hours. The route climbs a total of 9,050ft (2,578m) and drops 15,205ft (4,634m). The altitude varies between 1,000 and 7,430ft (305 and 2,264m); it crosses the spectacular steep cliffs and rocky paths of the Sierra Nevada and through the deep canyons of Squaw Valley. Horse and rider have to endure extreme heat – 100°F (35°C) or more in high humidity.

There are four halts, one of half an hour and three of an hour (this time is not included in the 24 hours limit). Vets examine each horse approximately ten times, and if it does not pass any test it must be withdrawn. Twelve hours after the ride the first ten horses 'home' are examined again.

To win the Tevis Cup a horse must carry 74.8kg (165lb [11.7 stone]) and must finish fit to continue 'should the necessity arise'. The record time is 11 hours 39 mins! The horse which finishes in 'most superior condition to go on' and in the first ten wins the Haggin Cup. Those who finish within 21½ hours riding time and whose horses are 'fit to go on' are awarded Tevis Buckles, whatever weight they are carrying.

This event has shown that on average the Arab has far more stamina than any other breed – an incredible 90 per cent of the winners have been pure or half-bred Arabs. The most successful rider is Donna Fitzgerald who has won the Cup five times with the same Arab horse.

Long distance riding in America is organised by the American Endurance Ride Conference and the North American Trail Ride Conference, who run endurance and competitive rides. ERs are races with no maximum speed limit; there is an annual North American Endurance Championship. Competitive rides vary in speed and distance, but are usually shorter than ERs.

The AERC was formed in 1971 and began with just 24 rides; now it has over 600, with a membership of over 2,500. Distances vary from 25 to 100 miles (40 to 150km), with 50 miles the most popular. Rides often have exciting names like 'Joe's Dugout XP' and 'Death Valley Encounter'.

Rides for the AERC Championship are 50 and 100 miles (80 and 160km), running from April to November with awards for turnout and performance. There is no grading and riders can start with a 100 mile (160km) ride if they want to.

Many more young people are taking up long-distance riding and getting a lot of pleasure from it (Steve Moore)

In America it's 'anything goes' as far as clothing is concerned, and riders are permitted to wear running shoes – over hilly terrain they frequently dismount and run directly behind the horse, hanging onto his tail to ascend steep hills or mountains. This helps to conserve the horse's energy and reduce his heart rate, particularly useful when approaching a vet gate. Horses are also allowed to have hoof pads, and many competitors use them for any ride which is particularly rocky. Neither pads nor running shoes are allowed in Europe.

AUSTRALIA

Australia's most prestigious ride, held over 100 miles (160km) and to be ridden in one day, is the Tom Quilty Endurance Ride; it is also Australia's National Championship Ride. Tom Quilty was a tough bushman who helped launch the sport, and the first ride started at 1.14am on 1 October 1966 with a field of 26 horses and riders.

For 20 years the ride was held in the Blue Mountains of Sydney. It is considered to be one of the toughest in the world with steep mountain terrain, overflowing creeks, clay-pan areas, quick sand, drops and hills. In recent years the ride has moved from state to state. In 1986 it was held in Gawler, north of Adelaide, South Australia; in 1987 it was held in Tasmania, where, despite the 14-hour long boat trip from the mainland, it attracted 79 competitors. In 1988 it was held in Queensland. Entries are around the 100 mark.

Successful riders in this event include Jenny Oliver on Glenallan Soloman, particularly outstanding because she has won three consecutive Quiltys; Bernard Harris, whose horse was the first to win the 'Fittest Horse Award'; and Betty Serpell who has earned herself the title of 'Quilty Queen' as she has completed more Quilty rides than anyone else. Everyone who completes the ride wins one of the famous Tom Quilty Buckles, but to win the Tom Quilty Gold Cup the horse must pass the vet at the end of the ride.

Endurance riding in Australia has a different governing body for each state, but they are all governed by the Australian Endurance Riders' Association (AERA). Unlike UK rules, there is a minimum weight of 73kg (161lb [11½ stone]) – not much fun for a light-weight rider, although there is a lightweight division in competition classes.

The sport is popular in New Zealand too and the north and south have Championships: the North over 100km (62½ miles), and the South over 100 miles (160km) in two days.

Pauline Holloway and Silver Zora crossing one of the many streams on Exmoor
(Bob Langrish)

EUROPE

ELDRIC – the European Long Distance Rides Conference – was formed in 1979 to meet the need for minimum and standard requirements at international rides, since national rules varied considerably as did standards of veterinary care. It hoped to encourage international competition by promoting and co-ordinating suitable rides, and by setting standards for veterinary rules. There are twelve members: Austria, Belgium, France, Germany, Great Britain, Holland, Italy, Norway, Portugal, Sweden, Switzerland.

The concept of an international long distance riding conference was born at a meeting in London in 1978. The German Endurance Riding Association (VDD), with Mr H. Stricker as president and Mrs Penelope Dauster as vice president, agreed to support such a conference. In the following year a meeting at the Equitana Exhibition was attended by delegates and observers from ten national long distance riding associations representing seven countries. A declaration of intent was signed, agreeing on minimum requirements for rides. An appeal was made to the FEI asking them to simplify the crossing of horses across European frontiers. (ELDRIC was not in competition with the FEI which at that time had no interst in endurance riding.)

The next ELDRIC meeting was also held in 1979 by the French Endurance Riding Society (CNREE), and laid down proper rules for a European points championship – now known as the European Trophy – which was to held for the first time in 1980.

Welfare of the horse is considered most important and ELDRIC is concerned with achieving the best possible conditions for the animal, before, during and after the competition. Another important function is to encourage communication between the member countries and to help make information widely available.

The European Trophy has been awarded on a points basis since 1980 and has a challenge comparable to World and European Championships. ELDRIC Trophy rides must either be FEI rides against the clock, or must fulfil the ELDRIC minimum requirements. Each country may organise a maximum of four rides counting towards the Trophy, and points are awarded according to the rider's placing and the kilometres ridden – the two figures are then added together. Only the best three rides will count for the trophy and at least one ride must be abroad. The rider must be a member of either the EHPS or the BHS, and the horse must be aged six or over. Types of saddlery and rider clothing are optional (there are no rules about hats).

Obligatory veterinary inspections include a pre-ride check, checks during the ride, and checks at the finish. On rides up to and including 100km per day the final check takes place not less than an hour after the finish; on longer rides the final check will be five hours or so after the finish. Rides may be subject to dope tests.

In 1987 there were 29 ELDRIC rides over a total of nearly 3,000 miles (4,410km) in ten countries. British rides run under ELDRIC rules include Breamore, Summer Solstice, Red Dragon, and Goodwood. Nineteen riders from seven countries competed successfully in the 1987 ELDRIC Trophy, and the winner was Denis Pesce from Germany on his Selle Français horse Malfenik.

· EUROPEAN CHAMPIONSHIPS ·

The 1985 European Championships were held in the beautiful countryside around Rosenau in Austria. Teams from seven countries – Austria, France, Germany, Great Britain, Hungary, Italy and the USA, plus individuals from Switzerland – took part in the 100 miles (160km) ride. Hilde Jarc of Austria became the European Champion on her Arab Samum, and the team winners were France (Michel Laracine, Christian Merkle, Marie Lux); Great Britain was third.

The 1987 European Championships were held in Erlangen, Germany, but the ride unfortunately suffered bad weather, continual rain hampering riders as they tackled the 103 mile (approx) (166km) route. Forty-two horses from three continents (Asia, Europe and North America) took part and eleven countries started. A French rider won the European title – Gaston Mercier on Mao IV; second was Liz Finney for Great Britain with Show Girl II, and team winners were America.

· *FEI* ·

The FEI (Fédération Équestre Internationale) is the international authority for equestrian sports; it approves regulations and sanctions FEI rides, and its members are national federations. ELDRIC is represented on the FEI sub-committee and both organisations collaborate closely. The FEI first drew up rules for endurance riding in 1983, and held its first rides in 1984.

Rules have the same minimum requirements as ELDRIC's; furthermore, if a ride is to be sanctioned by the FEI, it must have entrants only with permission from their National Federation. An FEI ride can be run as an ELDRIC ride and vice versa if the conditions are fulfilled.

FEI rules allow allow that riders from outside Europe may compete in European rides on borrowed horses. The loans are normally reciprocal – ie a horse is lent in exchange for a ride abroad.

WORLD CHAMPIONSHIPS

The first World Endurance Championships took place near Rome in September 1986. Forty-nine horses from three different continents and eleven nations took part at the site of the 1960 Olympic Games in Pratoni del Vivaro. It was held over 160 km (100 miles). There were check halts of one hour after 40, 80 and 120km and vet gates after 100 and 140km.

Many were eliminated because of the combination of fast speeds in high temperatures and high humidity – only 14 finished the ride successfully. The individual winner was Cassandra Schuler of America with an average speed of 14.8kmph; nine national teams took part, and the team Gold was won by Great Britain.

3 The Right Horse

All types of horses have been able to prove themselves in long distance riding. Unlike other equestrian sports where only a certain 'type' is expected to succeed, this opens its doors to most. Cobs and ponies can complete the 100 mile (160km) distance as well as the Arab so long as they are sufficiently fit.

Whatever the breed, a calm, generous temperament is more important than breeding and conformation. It's no good having a horse which wastes a lot of energy messing about. Any horse will be excited on a ride, but he must be able to settle down into a good pace and listen to his rider. He ought to be interested in what is around him and enjoy the adventure every bit as much as his rider. Arriving at the finish, he should be as fresh in outlook as he was when he started – it would be awful to have a horse which was really miserable and only picked up towards the end because he realised the ride was over.

You don't want a fiery horse but you do need one with a bit of spirit, as courage could make all the difference on a tough ride. He must behave reasonably well in company but should not fret too much when asked to work solo. It is a great advantage if the horse will take the lead as well as follow – many have an annoying tendency to slow up when away from others. You can do little to alter a horse's mental attitude. For instance, a placid horse when you start feeding it up and getting it fit may become quite unmanageable.

The horse/rider relationship is very important in long distance riding. Quite often a special bond is formed and communication becomes almost telepathic. The horse should be totally responsive to the aids. If you want to slow up, even if others are going on, it should be obedient enough to do so. And if you happen to part company, he should stop and wait for you to recover. This is where voice commands come into their own. Many riders find that after a while they can ride by voice alone. Provide the horse with a bit of variety, too, either in the winter, or between rides – many horses enjoy jumping.

There are sometimes special attributes which will put one horse ahead of another. For instance, a horse could have a natural physical capacity for endurance which may well have come about through his breeding. Some are born athletes which need little fitness training and have very low resting pulse rates. Horses like this are very lucky finds and much valued by their riders.

Soundness is vital and is often a characteristic of native blood, Arab or Thoroughbred crossed with Welsh for example. Natives are renowned

Val Long and her Arab stallion Tarim, one of the sport's most successful combinations
(Bob Langrish)

*'No, I think we should go this way!' Janet Maddock and her Arab gelding Sueh
(Bob Langrish)*

for being tough and hardy, with sensible temperaments. Smaller, more compact horses tend to stay sound, and find it easier to carry themselves. But heavy- or lightweight, any horse should be able to cope given the right training.

CONFORMATION

On rides where the terrain is uneven and difficult good conformation is important so that the horse can move freely and in such a way that he will not tire or injure himself. A horse with straight, well-matched limbs and correctly formed joints will be better balanced and less likely to suffer strain and sprain. Being well proportioned he has a more efficient structure which should help him to a good performance. If the horse is put together well, sustained riding will not cause him any harm. Many faults can be tolerated in shorter distances at slower speeds, but when demands are increased to cover greater distances and involving extra stress, the faults can manifest themselves in injury and weakness. It is important that his construction allows him to move easily over hilly or rough terrain, and keep going for several hours.

Looks do not necessarily matter – some unlikely looking horses are good because of their generous and hardy spirit. But the rider who aims for the top will need to invest in a good horse. This will undoubtedly mean paying a higher price, an expense which will very likely pay off, in the saving of future vets' fees, wasted entry fees and disappointment.

Here is a brief explanation of the term 'conformation': it concerns the way the horse is put together, that is, the skeleton, and muscle structures around it, and their relation to one another as a whole. It concerns shape and proportions. No one feature should dominate the rest, and all 'component parts' should be in proportion and work together harmoniously. Anything faulty, which spoils the natural symmetry, is a potential weakness – if put under stress, this will be the first part to give way. A fault with a foreleg for instance could result in a joint being placed under a great deal of stress when being ridden. The physical action, together with the extra weight of the rider, will set up a form of chain reaction involving firstly the joint, and then the ligaments and muscles. Weak hocks could give rise to uneven strains down the leg, perhaps even causing foot problems.

To evaluate the horse's conformation you need to step back from him a pace or two and assess his general appearance. The overall picture you gain ought to be one of harmony and a good horse will have a 'presence' – something about him which makes him stand out but which is hard to define. He should be alert and keen, and his physique should be compact and balanced. The ideal endurance horse should not incline to fat. The horse with a lighter frame is more suitable for long distance riding.

What might strike you first about the horse is his head. A large good eye implies a generous or kind horse; a small 'piggy' eye can denote a bad temper. A touch of white in the eye is not necessarily bad; it is a characteristic of Appaloosas, and wall eyes are often found in cream and coloured horses (this is simply due to a lack of pigment in the iris). Look for calm, large eyes and ears which are alert and mobile.

It doesn't particularly matter what shape head an endurance horse has, be it well-bred or common, but a good-sized nostril is a good prerequisite as the horse breathes solely through his nose and when ridden at speed he will need to fill his lungs to their full capacity. There should be room for the width of a hand in the throatlash area, between the cheek bones, to give plenty of breathing room.

The head should not be too heavy. In partnership with the neck it acts as a sort of pendulum against the rest of the body: the horse moves by lifting his head and neck up, shifting his weight to the rear as he does so, then transferring the weight to the front by lowering them. A heavy head would be heavy on the forehand, and probably the rider's hands too. So, for balance and therefore endurance, a light head on a medium-shaped neck is preferable. Where the head meets neck the junction should not make a thick throat as this could give rise to respiration problems. This is usually a fault of horses with short thick necks and upright shoulders. A guiding standard for the length of the neck is for it to be equal to one and a half times the length of the head as measured from the poll to the lowest part of the upper lip. (This does not apply to stallions due to their crested necks.)

A good shoulder is vital for a potential endurance horse. It is the length and angle of the shoulders which determine the length of stride and potential for extending stride. The ideal is a long shoulder, which slopes at an angle of 45 degrees or slightly more in relation to the ground, combined with a short and upright upper arm, short cannon, and a long/medium length pastern, which reflects the angle of the shoulder.

The angle of the humerus, connecting the shoulder with the upper arm at the radius, can also be crucial. A good shoulder can be spoiled if the humerus is too short because the foreleg will be closer to the front, resulting in a short stride and greater knee action, causing concussion in the leg. If it is too long, the elbow and foreleg will be tucked into the chest, and could cause the girth to chafe behind the elbow. A correctly short humerus together with a good shoulder means that the foreleg will be in the correct angle at the front, giving the horse a greater ability to lengthen the stride and have a free action. With this conformation the horse is less likely to suffer concussion damage in the forelimbs, and a long sloping shoulder allows plenty of room for muscle to develop during training. A straight shoulder will cause the horse to have shorter strides and oblige him to work twice as hard.

Avoid horses with narrow chests because the forelegs will be close to-gether causing interference at the joints. Such horses have the tendency to 'plait' – the forelegs (or hind legs) cross over one another. To evaluate the relationship between the chest and legs, stand in front of the horse and visualise a line from the point of the shoulder to the ground. It should pass through the centre of the knee, fetlock and foot. Anything outside this line suggests faults which will lead to poor action. A good width of chest will ensure that the horse has plenty of room to accommodate his lungs when in their full capacity.

The horse has eight pairs of true ribs attached to the vertebrae and sternum, and ten pairs of false ribs which are attached to the vertebrae only. The true ribs are flat in comparison to the false ribs which should be well sprung. Arabs have an extra pair of ribs, making a total of nine-teen, with five lumbar vertebrae instead of six. The false ribs cover the kidneys and other vital organs and need to be fairly long – if flat and short the horse's shape will tend to allow the saddle to slip back, particularly when riding over hilly country.

There are a number of faults in the conformation of the back to watch out for. One of the worst is a roach back (convex in outline) because it results in a short stride; the horse may also be prone to forging – catching the toe of the hind shoe against the underside of the toe of the forefoot.

The back should not be too hollow; a reasonably high wither will help prevent the saddle from slipping forwards, though too high and it will cause problems with saddle fitting.

A longer back will be an advantage when it comes to speed because it allows the hindlegs to be brought further forward under the body, producing a longer stride. A short back, though obviously stronger, may have the opposite effect and be less able to absorb concussion. However, if too long the result is a weak loin or poor quarters, causing weak hindlegs.

The loin, the area between the saddle and croup, needs to be strong and its muscles powerful. The horse's hindlegs depend on the strength to be found here, and as the loin covers the vital organs it also needs to be fairly broad.

We now move along to the quarters, the horse's powerhouse. Here lies the key to rhythmic and effortless strides. The quarters should appear to be round at the top, a pear shape widening into muscular second thighs. Hips ought not to stick out and they must be level. A dropped hip usually means that the horse has suffered damage and may result in unevenness of gait. A horse with poor thighs combined with a thin, under-developed gaskin will be weak in the hindquarters, and is likely to have irregularities in the hindlegs as a result.

Good hocks are very important, and their relation to the quarters and hindleg overall is critical to the horse's performance. The hock is perhaps the hardest worked joint in the horse's body. If the point of hock is in line with the chestnut, there should be greater efficiency with the least risk of strain. Ideally, the second thigh must be long and the hock set low, keeping the hind cannon short. A vertical line should connect the point of the buttock with the point of hock, and carry on down the back of the cannon bone. This should give maximum leverage for all the parts of the leg and help to provide greater speed.

Common faults found in the hocks include sickle hocks which, looking at the horse broadside on, are curved on the front surface, and hocks that are carried out of the above mentioned vertical line. Both faults give rise to uneven wear and extra strain, and perhaps a lack of propulsive power, since the hocks cannot engage fully under the body. A hock which is too straight will have the same defects. Looking at the tail, bowed hocks are where the points, 'bow' outwards and the lower leg is carried inwards;

cow hocks are the opposite and both reduce speed as the limbs are unable to move straight, so the animal is likely to have uneven wear in the joint. In order to absorb the concussion properly and to cope with the weight, hock joints need to be large, and a matching pair.

To judge good conformation in a foreleg it is best to look at the horse from the front and to view the legs as a pair. Also, look at the degree of straightness between legs and body – if they are out of line, undue strain will be placed on the leg and may cause lameness.

The elbow must be clear of the ribs for the movement of the leg to be free – if the elbow is so close to the ribs that you cannot get a fist between the upper leg and body, the elbow is said to be 'tied in' and the shoulder movement will be restricted. If the elbow is set further back, the spine, and the rider too, will be subjected to extra concussion, and any fault in the elbow will also place the hocks under extra strain.

The upper leg needs to be strong and well muscled, and the knee set as low as possible on short, strong cannon bones.

Knees, as with hocks, need to be large and flat and must be a pair. One of the worst faults is 'calf knee', or 'back at the knee' where the leg curves behind and below the knee; it causes tendon problems and is useless at absorbing concussion. Another fault is known as 'tied in below the knee', that is, when the measurement around the bone immediately below the knee is less than that taken nearer the fetlock joint. This results in a constriction of the tendons. 'Over the knee' is when the cannon bone slopes back from below the knee so that the knee seems to be knuckling over; this seems to have no bad effects and such horses rarely have tendon problems.

Now we come to the subject of *bone*. Measurement of bone, together with the horse's general build, is one way to judge the weight-carrying ability of a horse: this is usually done by measuring the circumference of the cannon bone. Bone is a tube-like structure with marrow at its centre. The smaller or narrower the centre, the stronger the bone. Its density, as opposed to the height of the horse, dictates the capacity to carry weight and cope with stress. A good circumference (at least 8in) indicates good bone.

It is a failing for the knee to be too high off the ground since a long cannon indicates structural weakness. The strongest is a short, thick cannon, which is the same width the whole way down. The fetlock joint should be large and well-formed.

Moving down the leg we come to the horse's shock absorbers – his pasterns. Short, upright pasterns can jar the legs and lead to a variety of unsoundnesses; too long, and the pastern is a potential weakness, though length does provide a comfortable ride. The hind pastern needs to be a little shorter than that of the foreleg because of the flexing action of the hock, but both fore and hind pasterns must be at the same angle as the foot.

One of the most important parts of the horse is the foot, and it is perhaps the first thing one should look at when assessing a potential long distance riding horse. However, see chapter 7 for the foot in greater detail.

ACTION

The way the horse moves is of prime importance if he is going to be doing long distance work, and action is very much related to conformation. The ideal is a horse that has a long, ground-covering stride and free, effortless movement, and if he is well put together he will move well too. Limbs should be carried in a straight line and each joint should be flexed properly – you ought to be able to see the sole of each foot during each stride. You can best judge action by standing to the front or to the rear of the horse and then watch him being walked or trotted up. And, looking sideways on, check that the poll and the quarters remain level as the horse moves.

Some horses, often due to conformational deficiency, have a tendency to interfere – to hit one limb with another. A horse that can cope quite adequately with shorter rides may start to interfere when more is asked of him on longer, faster rides. It may also occur if the horse is not fit enough, or when over-tired, or through bad riding.

For similar reasons a horse may brush, where the fetlock, or sometimes coronet, knock one against the other; ill-fitting or heavy shoes may also cause brushing. If this happens during training use either brushing or Yorkshire boots. Fitting a feathered shoe is also a solution.

Speedy cutting is when one leg or foot strikes into the opposite leg just below the knee, causing a more severe wound. It is fairly rare and usually happens when an unfit horse encounters heavy going.

Over-reaching is when the toe of the hind shoe strikes into the back of the foreleg, usually the heel area; it can also be caused when going at speed over heavy going, or by careless riding, and can often result in the loss of a shoe. Use an over-reach boot, and your farrier could fit special hind shoes (see p117).

Forging occurs when the toe of the hind shoe strikes the underneath surface of the front shoe directly ahead of it. It can be the result of over-sloping pasterns or again of bad riding. This fault can also be overcome by remedial shoeing (see p116).

Undercutting can result from a very compact or short-backed conformation and the type of action that results. As the foreleg comes up from the ground, the toe of the front foot scrapes the toe of the hind foot; to prevent further injury the front feet should have square-toed shoes fitted, using a bevelled-off shoe with two clips. The fore foot should then miss the toe of the hind.

AGE

In general, the minimum age for a horse beginning long distance riding is five. Four-year-olds may be allowed to take part in pleasure rides, while five-year-olds may be permitted to compete in Novice competitions (BHS) for the minimum of a year.

There seems to be no upper age limit. Horses and ponies have proved that they can go on competing into their twenties. It all depends on how the animal has been ridden in the past. To continue until that age every care must have been taken not to rush the horse or push him too hard, too soon, making sure he is fully prepared for what is asked of him. Some good horses have been 'ruined' in this sport because riders were too anxious to 'get on'.

BREEDS

The Arab horse has without doubt proved itself to be the best breed for long distance riding; it seems made for it! In America and Australia Arabs have taken the top placings in most of the national endurance races. They cope well with the very high temperatures and humid climate and are bred for endurance.

Large numbers of the breed compete in Britain – pure-breds, Anglo-Arabs and part-breds. One competitor once commented that she often had to remind herself that she was at a long distance ride and not an Arab Horse Society event!

The Arab's background explains its success: for centuries it carried the Bedouin, enduring a harsh climate and rough terrain, travelling long distances with only meagre food rations. Endurance riders who have Arabs marvel at their capacity and courage, and the horses themselves seem to become 'passionate' about the sport, relishing every ride.

The Arab has natural qualities of soundness and stamina, and its fans claim that its temperament combines courage and fire with gentleness, kindness, and good sense. Another advantage is that it gives a comfortable, light ride.

The Thoroughbred, is less suitable since it can be delicate in constitution, more prone to unsoundness and takes a little more skill to keep;

Becky Broughton (aged eight), one of the youngest riders in the sport, having successfully competed at Rainworth CTR with Kimberley (Sue Parslow)

it has quick reactions which can result in scattiness, so it is less likely to settle and this might even prevent you from starting if excitement has pushed the heart rate up. The Thoroughbred is really bred to race at speed, though some have inherited that 'staying power' which will keep them going no matter what. The breed also tends to have shallow and sensitive feet which bruise easily.

The Thoroughbred, then, requires a capable and knowledgeable rider, and is certainly not for the novice. However, when crossed with a native breed, the Thoroughbred produces a good prospect – Connemara or New Forest cross, Welsh, Highland or Irish Draught. Native blood has the effect of calming the hot Thoroughbred temperament, adding 'bone' and substance, and hopefully native hardiness and soundness.

PONIES

Ponies and pony crosses provide the economy of easy management together with good temperament. More and more adult riders are choosing to compete with the larger breeds – Welsh Cobs, New Forest crosses – and the same maxims regarding suitability apply. Like horses, some conformational defects can be lived with provided that the pony does not injure itself or give an uncomfortable ride. The ability to do well on the poorest of grazing has developed through the generations, together with a true hardiness and ponies are likely to be very sound in feet, limbs and wind.

Although sometimes wilful, they can be intelligent, sensible and easy going and are more likely to be sure-footed – some have a sort of sixth sense ability to avoid boggy ground, and in this case 'listen' to your mount, give him the reins and allow him to choose the route.

Many 'all-round' family ponies successfully turn their hooves to long distance riding; it provides change from schooling work and will rejuvenate even the old 'school-master' pony who has worked for so long giving the same old lessons.

BREED PORTRAITS
· *THOROUGHBRED* ·

Margaret Swords has competed with her registered Thoroughbred gelding Kelston Salamanca (15.3hh) since 1985, competing in CTRs and ERs. In both 1986 and 1987 they were seventh in the EHPS list of national top ten horses over the season.

Margaret says of her horse:

He was highly nervous, and excitable during all of his first season and it has taken three years to achieve peak fitness, mentally and physically and to teach him to relax and save energy. He is still sometimes 'overwhelmed' by horses overtaking, and hard to settle again afterwards.

His heart rate is naturally quite low when resting (34/36) but because of his temperament he tends to take longer than half-an-hour to switch off mentally and so rarely vets out after the ride below 42 which is annoying for grading purposes.

IIe prefers to canter but has a good trot and can usually be persuaded to keep it up for quite long periods. He finds CTR speeds too slow – he paces himself best at about 10mph (16km). He is very calm about travelling, shoeing, vetting and so on, and is never worried by strange objects or noises. Steep hill work makes him panic and he scrambles; so does heavy clay or bog when he can't move his feet normally.

Unfortunately his feet are small, and one is inclined to be boxy; they won't take a heavy shoe which is a problem because he is hard on shoes and we have a lot of roads – they don't grow very quickly either, so I am loath to have him shod too often. The quality of the actual horn is good and not brittle. His soles are good too, and only rarely does he 'feel' a stone.

On the whole he is an easy horse to keep but is difficult to ride because of that racehorse fifth gear which needs a good half mile to stop, and his excitability. But he is intelligent, he has perfect stable manners, and is a wonderful friend on a long ride. He has certainly been a challenge, and in the long run well worth it, but perhaps not one I would recommend to everyone.

· *ARAB* ·

Hanwary is Pat Payne's 15.1hh Arab gelding (Crabbet bred). Aged ten he is in his third year in long distance riding, competing in Open EHPS CTRs. She bought him as an eight-year-old:

He did some pleasure rides with me when he was eight, and 17 Novice rides when he was nine. In his tenth year, he started Open rides, 25 to 40 miles.

There was a bit of a problem initially, which is why I did the pleasure rides, because he was flighty. The first thing I did was to teach him to trot on a loose rein – in the Novice rides I stuck at trot and didn't canter until he had settled down. By the end of his fifth pleasure ride there were no problems. He's quite level-headed and he really enjoys going on a ride.

Last year (1987) he did really well, and won the EHPS Highpoint Novice Trophy, ten grade ones and seven grade twos. This year (1988) he has got grade twos, threes and fours in Open rides.

Arabs are criticised for being highly strung, but I think that if you treat them 'normally' they act normally. He is sweet-tempered and good in traffic – I have kept him quite versatile, which I think is important if he is going to travel and be ridden in different areas.

His resting pulse rate is 28–29, but when he's out on a ride his starting pulse rate will be about 30–36, and after the ride it has been about 42.

His feet are very good – apparently some Arabs tend to have contracted feet.

Hanwary's training is divided into four different categories: a working and schooling ride, a pleasure hack, a long distance ride done either for distance or speed, and interval training. Pat also takes him on a day ride. She explains:

> I think it is important that the horse is prepared to take me out for the whole day, for eight or nine hours, as he would in a competition. This helps with his fitness but also makes sure that he is mentally up to it.
>
> I don't think it's a good idea to give horses a complete rest from October to Christmas. They are not worked hard every day, and it seems unfair just to abandon the bond that has grown between you. I keep him just ticking over through the winter, and in January to February time I start work with him. If you let your horse get completely soft over the winter you have to spend so much time getting him fit.

· HEAVYWEIGHT COB ·

Jumbo's story just goes to show that a horse deemed 'totally unsuitable' can succeed. Jumbo belongs to Beryl Dean and is an Irish half-bred. When he was 14 a vet diagnosed arthritis and advised destruction. Fortunately, Beryl disagreed and found a solution – work, work and more work. Since then he has clocked up almost 1,000 miles, 800 of those in competition, and is fitter than ever.

> We have specialised in 50 mile (80km) rides, CTRs at 8mph; when you start going up to 100 mile (160km) rides you need to spend more time in training. I have always worked full time so Jumbo has only been ridden at weekends. He'll have perhaps three or four weeks off in December, but otherwise I ride him in the winter. When he was younger I used to ride him 25 miles each Saturday, then he would be ready to build up and extend to 30 or 40 miles (64km) in the spring.

Horses of heavier build find it harder to cope with hills and like many others Jumbo is not at his best when it is hot.

> He finds it difficult to cope with the heat – I wouldn't do a 50 mile (80km) ride if I thought it was going to be hot. He performs best in spring, autumn and winter.

Jumbo has proved himself fitter than ever – on a ride in his 19th year his heart rate was 40 at the start of the ride, and 42 at the finish.

> He's completely the wrong sort though. Even when I bought him he was unsuitable, but there were more of his sort when we started long distance riding, and now there are far more Arab types.

· QUARTER HORSE ·

Diablo Prairiegold is one of a small number of Quarter horses to have taken part in long distance riding. He is a 14.2hh gelding and belongs

Proving that a Quarter horse is truly versatile, Carolyn Shackles' Diablo Prairiegold tackles the open moorland on Exmoor (Bob Langrish)

to Carolyn Shackles. He started long distance riding in 1985 and stayed in Novice classes into 1986, competing in BHS and EHPS up to 25 miles. Carolyn says:

We started in 1987 in Bronze Buckle qualifiers and went into Open classes in EHPS – we did the Final at Leicester in July in 85 degrees Fahrenheit, and then came out and did a Bronze Buckle ride the week after at Telford, which proved he could handle the heat!

We started 1988 with a Bronze Buckle at Monks Kirby which was tough and nearly put us off for life! Then the Gold qualifier at Weston Park, with Wantage two-day ride soon after that.

As is characteristic of the breed, Diablo Prairiegold is very versatile. He has competed successfully in show jumping, cross country, Western riding, and hunts during the winter. He has been High Point Horse at the Quarter Horse Show, won the Quarter Horse Versatility twice in the last six years, and was second in the remaining four.

He is a very easy horse to feed, competing on very little. He will always eat away from home and loves to go away to places. He has a typical Quarter horse temperament, loves people, and to be fussed. He is forward-going but he does not hot up and will go along at the pace I choose. As with all Quarter horses, as soon as you drop the reins he goes like 'an old donkey'. Pick up the reins and you have all the speed and power you will ever want. A Quarter horse derives its name from being the fastest horse in the world over a quarter of a mile.

His heart rate is 34 to 40/60, and comes back lower at 50 miles than 25 miles. He has a dust allergy which prevents it coming right back. He is finding CTRs slow and hates having to slow down – he averages a Golden Horseshoe qualifier at $9^{1}/_{2}$ mph.

He is very good with any terrain. I think this is partly because he was hunted for six years, it certainly teaches horses to look after themselves, and he loved Exmoor.

He is a very sound little horse; the only trouble I have is with bruised soles but this is not a breed fault as my other purebred Quarter horse does not suffer with them. He is kind and an easy ride for anyone. He has a sense of humour and will play you up, but would never throw you off. He is very intelligent and gets bored very easily so he needs a lot of variety.

Quarter horses are a very compact, muscular breed. They have a lot of Thoroughbred in them, crossed with Spanish stock and their agility and good temperament make them excellent riding horses. Their average height is around 14.2hh to 15.2hh but they carry a man very well being deep-girthed.

I would recommend one to anyone, you would never get a better friend.

· WELSH SECTION B ·

Cawdor Honey has helped to put ponies on the map in long distance riding, and her owner, Jan Lloyd-Rogers is very proud of her achievements. 13.2hh Honey, a former show pony and brood mare, started long distance riding aged 13 and has had 4 successful years in the sport – she was the fittest horse out of 90 competitors on the 100 mile (160km) Red Dragon ride. Her achievements include 9th place in the Summer Solstice, the Rosy Memorial 500 mile trophy, and awards for best pony for the Red Dragon, and best native pony.

Jan believes that ponies have been badly under-rated in the sport and feels that lightweight adults would do well to consider a pony whose attributes include a good, even temperament, and inherent soundness and sure-footedness.

When fit Honey's resting pulse rate is 36 and comes back to between 38 and 42 after a ride. She is ridden in a snaffle and although she can be strong, Jan is able to drop the reins on a ride and the pony will maintain her pace.

She has got the most superb temperament, she will pass any traffic and will tackle any obstacles on rides – others wait for us to come along for a lead across bridges and so on! She is exceptionally sure-footed. I think ponies can be super for adults but it is important that the pony's temperament suits the adult.

4 The Right Rider

QUALITIES

The qualities needed by those who take part in long distance rides are by no means exclusive and can be found or achieved by almost any one. No particularly special skills are needed, and the rider does not need any special training, simply a competent level of horsemanship. The sport offers the chance to ride in some of the most beautiful and scenic areas of the country, and there is plenty of scope for the rider with ambition who can work up through the lower distance competitive trail rides to the 100 mile (160km) ride and thence on to endurance rides. Opportunities to ride abroad in challenging competitions may follow, perhaps in European or World Championships. And who knows, endurance riding may soon become an Olympic sport.

Understanding your own horse is one of the most valuable skills in the long distance rider. You must be able to judge how he is coping with a particular situation, to know when he is tired and when he is capable of going on, and to recognise his limitations. You may have to decide whether in his eagerness to keep up with others he is in fact doing himself harm and be ready to alter ride tactics accordingly. Just because the horse finished well in the same ride the year before, does not necessarily mean he will repeat the same performance, and it can be a hard decision to make if you are up with a crowd of riders and you have to break away and let them go on. If you carry on you may risk the horse becoming exhausted but if you slow down you could at least complete the ride. But long distance riding is all about good horsemanship and producing horses that are fit and in good condition so that they finish their rides sound.

Your stable management skills in general need to be of a good standard too. It is obviously important to keep your horse in the best way possible. Whether the horse is kept in or out, a good basic daily routine and a sensible long-term policy are essential. This should include good feeding, having a good farrier who will take regular care of the horse's feet, regular worming, keeping vaccinations up to date, and so on. Good standards in stable management are the best foundation for whatever you choose to do with your horse.

Competing is more likely to be successful if you have a good team behind you. This could include your family who will give you moral support, and your helper who accompanies you to rides. But it should also include those professionals without whom you might not even be able to make those entries in the first place – your vet, your farrier and perhaps your saddler. Choose each one wisely – your horse deserves the

(page 43) Tackling a steep hill (Bob Langrish)

A crew set to work tacking up a horse at the end of a half-way halt, ready for the rider to set off again (Bob Langrish)

best, even at a high price. Discuss any problems you have with them, their advice could prove very valuable.

On a personal level a good long distance rider needs to be calm and sensible – it is quite true that the way the rider is feeling is quickly transmitted to the horse. Excitement or panic will quickly be picked up and the horse will respond likewise, which is not the best frame of mind to be in when out on a ride.

You need to be fairly organised to plan a useful fitness training programme for your horse, spanning up to three months, and competition calendar; these organisational skills will also come in handy when you load up your car or horse box the night before a competition – that certain thing you leave behind could be crucial.

Patience is essential. Things don't always go to plan. There are times when your horse might be off work because of an injury and you have to wait until he's fully recovered – that may be of little comfort when you had a goal in sight but must wait until next season to achieve it. And it is wrong to push a youngster too much too soon, you could ruin a good horse. It all takes patience and determination. For riders who have had to retire a very successful horse it may also be hard to have to start again at the bottom with a new horse, but you must bring it up in the gradual way that it deserves.

RIDER SKILLS

You don't have to be a brilliant rider to compete in long distance riding, but you do need to be a very understanding and knowledgeable one, putting your horse first wherever you can. You need to be a considerate rider and have a feel for the horse and what he might be experiencing and what his reactions might be. It has been said that women riders are better at understanding horses because they are more sensitive, and that men are less good because they are so keen on achieving their aims: this is, however, a debatable point.

There's a lot to be said for riding 'positively'; the horse looks to his rider as the one in charge – it is you who has taken the place of the stallion at the head of the herd. If you are uncertain or afraid and he is left to himself, he will feel unsure and panicky. In new surroundings he will need you to tell him what to do. You must be able to make firm decisions and relay your intentions clearly to the horse.

Most horses will respond to wide open spaces and the company of others, and are quite different from the way they behave at home in the confines of their paddock. The horse will generally show more 'sparkle' and enthusiasm which sometimes bubbles over into naughtiness. When he is keen or fresh you must remember that he needs more direction from the rider who really must be positive and ride him forward. The legs should be kept on and the horse should be ridden into your rein contact.

Don't try and fight the horse – think of channelling his energy. If you continue to pull back he will probably throw his head up and become hollow backed, making it even harder to control him or to ride him correctly in any gait. Keep your legs on all the time, just a gentle pressure, so that the horse is continually reminded that you are in charge.

In this sport you must really work as a partnership, you can't just sit there like a sack of potatoes because in some cases you could be hindering the horse. It often pays to reappraise the way you ride. Get a friend to cast a critical eye over you while you ride; it may be that the way you are sitting is causing problems in the horse's back, making him as stiff as you are. Have some riding lessons – there's no shame in it, many top riders do. A freelance instructor would be only too pleased to teach you on your own horse at home.

A good rider should aim to be in balance with the horse at all times, placing his weight over the animal's centre of gravity and altering his position according to the speed of the horse. When standing, the horse's centre of gravity is just forward of the rider's knee, vertically beneath the horse's spine; as he goes faster, the centre of gravity moves forward, its exact location altering throughout the stride.

The centre of motion is located roughly in the saddle cantle area, just behind the rider's backside, so the rider really can use his seat and back to give either forward driving aids, or to 'hold' the horse. Usd correctly, your seat and posture can help keep the horse in a good rhythm and very little physical contribution besides this should be required.

You also need a deep seat, good balance and the ability to maintain a light contact with the horse's mouth at all paces. As you progress your horse will become accustomed to having less and less contact, which helps to minimise sores (lesions) and bruising at the mouth; you would be penalised for these at the end of the ride. Some riders have even adopted a form of neck reining so that they can keep the reins loose but still be in control.

The 'adoptive style' of the long distance rider is one which is long in the leg with knees flexible to act as a sort of shock absorber, and with loose contact on the reins so as to interfere with the horse as little as possible. The horse should go freely, carrying himself naturally with the least amount of involvement from the saddle. The key to this is achieving perfect balance and having a sympathy with the horse's movements. When riding over rough terrain and up and down hills, the endurance rider should hover above the horse's withers, giving the horse every opportunity to move freely.

The rider must be able to feel his horse's movements, hence the need for a saddle which will give close contact. You need to know how the horse is feeling – often you can feel tiredness coming on or the back beginning to stiffen up.

FITNESS

For distances longer than pleasure rides the rider must look at his or her own fitness. Fitness is the corner stone in this sport. The horse must be fit enough to cope with what is being asked of it so that it will not be placed under undue stress when distance and speed increase and the rider must also be fit. There is no point in having an ultra-fit horse if the rider gets tired. You want to get the best out of the horse and he may need all the help he can get, over tricky terrain and also when he gets to his 'sticking point' on the ride – then he will need plenty of encouragement, and fitness will give the rider the competitive edge.

Remember, the fitter you are, the easier it will be in those final miles when fatigue may make you weak and your muscles stiffen and ache. A tired rider is a cumbersome load for the horse and you may find you have to reduce your speed in order to maintain balance in the saddle. The rider may also become unco-ordinated, which upsets the horse's rhythm and sets up movement in opposition to his movements. This results in the rider gripping with his legs. When physically tired your concentration may go, and the horse and rider combination becomes very vulnerable. If you are fit you will be able to help him when he's tired, and guide him over rough terrain, minimising the risk of him injuring himself.

Many find that training and yardwork alone build up sufficient strength; others need to do a little more. A long distance rider needs to have a reasonable level of balance and suppleness, stamina and strength: stamina is fitness of the heart and lungs, improved by aerobic fitness; suppleness and strength will help you maintain the correct position in the saddle – if you are not supple your joints will tend to be stiff during a ride and therefore you are more susceptible to stresses and strains.

· WALKING ·

Walking is probably the best way to build up stamina. It is actually an aerobic activity, which will boost your staying power. That is, you will be able to perform the most strenuous activity – run further, ride harder – before you become breathless. Make it a brisk, purposeful walk: your pace needs to be fairly quick, swing your arms and fill your lungs with fresh air. Keep your back straight, your head up, and walk tall. Set a good rhythm and stride out!

Do this two or three times a week. The training principles for you are similar to those for your horse. Take your pulse and set yourself a target rate (see chart), checking your pulse regularly. Almost all the muscles are exercised when walking briskly – in the back, the abdomen, the upper arm and shoulder, hips, legs, chest – all except for the fore-arm. So it is the ideal exercise to combine with riding. It's also a good way of burning off any of that excess fat you might have at the beginning of the season.

· CHANGES ·

At rest, an average person will breathe about 10 litres of air per minute, but after 5 minutes of brisk walking this will have increased to around 40 or 50 litres. The oxygen extracted from this air will have risen from $\frac{1}{4}$ litre to more than $1\frac{1}{4}$ litres and the metabolic rate will have been increased by around five times.

There are great changes in the heart's capacity too. While at rest the heart pumps about 5 litres of blood each minute; during a brisk walk this can double, if not treble. The heart increases its output in two ways: by an increase in rate, and by increasing the stroke volume, that is, the amount it pumps at each beat. You could find that your pulse rate has doubled if you stop and check it after a brisk walking session.

To get the maximum benefit from your exercise programme you should work to between 60 and 80 per cent of your maximum heart rate. It is important to take your pulse before your exercise, and then afterwards when you have wound down and are at rest, when your heart rate should be back to normal.

So to calculate your personal heart training range you should first take your resting pulse rate. This is done by taking your pulse rate first thing in the morning, after a good night's sleep. Count how many heart beats there are in a full minute.

Using the following formula you can very simply work out your own personal training target heart rate, which is the criterion for all your exercise sessions:

220 (maximum heartbeats) - your age = your maximum heartbeats - your resting pulse = your heart rate reserve x .7 = 70 per cent of your heart rate reserve + your resting pulse = your target training heart rate. Divide by six for your ten second count.

To take your pulse take a watch with a second hand and place it on a table in front of you. Place three fingers of your right hand on the left wrist about 3cm below the mound of the thumb: this is where your radial artery is, and you should be able to feel the pulse and count the beats. It is usually easier to count to 15 seconds and multiply by four, or to 30 seconds and multiply by two.

In aerobic exercises oxygen is used to release energy from the chemical muscle fuels. Because walking is not as strenuous as some exercises – skipping for example – the fuels used are a mixture of carbohydrate and fat. Carbohydrate is in the form of blood sugar (glucose) and glycogen, which is the storage form of glucose in the muscle cell. Aerobic exercise benefits the heart, lungs, blood, blood vessels and muscle cells.

Aerobic fitness will also help raise your body's anaerobic threshold. Enzymes within the muscle cell extract energy from glucose and other enzymes in the liver, kidneys and elsewhere to remove lactic acid from the blood and recycle it back to glucose: this is the anaerobic system. By increasing the efficiency of your heart and lungs you reduce the need to use the anaerobic system.

So, grab your walking shoes and off you go. It shouldn't be too hard to fit walking into your daily or weekly routine. Perhaps you could get up a bit earlier and walk to the stables, or walk to work.

Aerobic activities include jogging, cycling, swimming, and of course, the aerobic class. If you choose to do exercises at home, don't forget to warm up properly or you could hurt your muscles.

· *HORSE WALKING* ·

Once a week why not lead your horse? After all, you need to practise trotting him up for the vet so walking would be an extension to this. At first he may find it very strange and will not be used to being led in a bridle, and you may find it a struggle to keep up with him and work in with his stride. On longer distance rides you may, like many riders, want to jump off and run alongside him to give him a break. He needs to know what you are doing, so when you get to that level it is advisable to run a mile or two with your horse as a part of your more advanced training.

· *EQUIPMENT* ·

Working with hand-, wrist- or ankle-weights, available from sports shops, will help you to bring your pulse rate up and get more out of your walking exercise.

Invest in a good pair of walking shoes or trainers. If you do need to walk and ride, you will obviously have to decide what footwear is best. You do need something with a heel (riding in training shoes is banned in Britain unless you have caged front enclosed stirrups). If you come to the conclusion that you should wear jodhpur or long riding boots, practise walking or running in them – really get them 'worn in' so that you avoid getting sore feet on the ride.

· *STRETCHING EXERCISES* ·

Simple daily stretching will help keep your body supple. When you get up in the morning reach up with your arms and stretch the spine. Or, why not limber up while preparing your horse for your ride: this involves a ten-minute work-out using all the major joints including the spine, Achilles muscles and tendons all likely to be made stiff by riding; these should be stretched before you ride in a series of suppling exercises which can easily be worked in with your actual riding routine.

It can begin with grooming your horse. For instance, start by brushing his face; stand with your legs slightly bent, brush five strokes with one hand and five with the other, stretching each arm as you do so, and giving a good brushing, so that your arms have a good 'work out'. As you turn to work down his near side, bend one knee and keep the other straight, stretched a little way behind it with the heel to the ground, stretching the calf muscles. Alternate legs as you move along and round to the off-side. Always do the horse's feet last, that way you will be warmed up enough to crouch down.

When mounted up, stand in the stirrups and stretch your heels down as far as they will go, each stretch to a count of eight . . .and then relax. Repeat the exercise two or three times.

Next, twist your upper body as far as you can to the left for eight counts, keeping your back as straight as possible, then to the right, and again left, and so on.

Now, stretch your arm and upper body forward to touch your horse's ears, then stretch back with your arm towards his tail; do this four times with each arm. Next raise your right arm above your head, then swing forward and downward to touch the right toe. Repeat with the left arm. It is important that your legs remain still – if you allow them to move backwards, the whole object of the exercise will be lost. Do this exercise four times.

To loosen your knee and ankle joints, try this exercise: remove both feet from the stirrups in turn, and swing your right lower leg backwards, bringing the heel upwards level with the horse's back, keeping your knee on the saddle. Repeat with the other leg. (If you are not sure how your horse might react to this, have a helper at his head.) Another is to remove each foot in turn from its stirrup and rotate both clockwise and anti-clockwise. Repeat with both feet simultaneously.

The following exercise will help you to improve your balance. Again, remove both feet from the stirrups, and lift both legs away from the horse's sides as far as you can, so that you are balancing almost entirely on your seat bones. You can do this at the halt and walk, and then at the trot as you become more proficient.

Now you should be limbered up and ready to warm your horse up before you start to work him. However, if your horse is very fresh when you first take him out, these exercises are likely to upset him. Instead, give and take with the reins. Give away the rein on one side while you stretch round to the opposite side with your upper body. Do the same on alternate sides. You could fit in the other stretching exercises later in your ride when the horse has settled.

As well as suppleness, the long distance rider will need strength – muscle power. People who have ridden and had horses all their lives will be quite strong in their arms and legs; years of conditioning, through riding, mucking out and hauling heavy buckets of water across a yard, will have seen to that.

Muscle strength in your upper body and legs will help you keep a good riding position throughout the hours you have to spend in the saddle and can be toned up by weight training. In a gym, supervisors will advise you on which exercises will benefit your riding muscles best, for instance calf-raises, leg-raises, sit-ups for the stomach, and so on. You will be recommended a régime which will work a whole spectrum of your body's muscles.

Walking, and swimming in particular will help to tone up muscles and in time, increase strength, depending on how hard you train. Any exercise, to be of benefit, must be done regularly, two or three times a week for example.

A ride day is likely to be a very long one. You will probably have an early start and a long journey; the actual ride will be physically tiring, but you won't be able to collapse in a heap afterwards – the horse's welfare is your responsibility, even if you do have a helper. Then there is the journey home and again the horse to see to. So, the fitter you can be, the better you will be able to cope with all of this.

And it should go without saying that the less excess weight you are carrying, the easier it will be for you to maintain fitness.

HELP YOUR HORSE

The long distance horse must be able to cope with a large variety of hazards. He must respond to varied terrain and weather conditions with equanimity and obedience. Plenty of training on home ground and on trips to unfamiliar places will help give your horse the experience he needs. This should include fording streams, riding through herds of cattle or sheep, pigs, busy roads, farmyards and machinery, plastic bags, and so on. Getting your horse to accept these things with indifference will be a real boon when you do meet them on a ride.

If you come across something that you think your horse will shy at, don't tense up because so will he – just sit quietly and ride him past. If you look ahead and totally ignore the object, the chances are he will too and your calmness will be communicated to him. However, if he does shy, ride him up to the object and allow him to inspect it.

Some horses have a great dislike for water. Find a friend whose horse is an 'old hand', then go to a stream, or better still a beach where you'll have plenty of space and can choose how deep to go. If you canter along together with your horse on the inside, away from the sea, you can gradually tease your horse into the water.

When riding into a stream keep close behind your lead horse – it's far better to do this than fight on your own, and it would certainly be

Being able to open and close gates of all types and sizes is one of a few vital skills (Steve Moore)

impossible if you got off and tried to drag the horse through. Choose a warm day, he won't be quite so miserable once he discovers he's got to get his feet wet. Some horses really enjoy splashing about in water — the more splash they make the better. But this may mean that his next plan is to get down and roll in it, so be careful! On a long distance ride streams can be an invaluable chance to cool the horse off a bit and allow him to have a drink.

Experience of riding in groups of other horses would be beneficial too, perhaps in the hunting field or on a local sponsored ride. Over-excitement in company will push the heart rate up and perhaps cause problems for you in veterinary inspections.

Being able to open and shut a gate quickly and without fuss could save you a lot of time. It just needs a bit of practice at home, and to make things easier your horse will need to be totally obedient to your legs. Good schooling in lateral movements (moving sideways from the leg) will be a great help. The horse must make a half pass to come up alongside the gate, stand square and still while it is unlatched, perform a turn on the forehand around the gate to the other side of it, do another half pass to close it, and stand still while the latch is re-fastened.

Basically, the way to tackle a gate is as follows: stand the horse parallel to the gate with his head just past the latch. Put your whip and reins into one hand, leaving the other free to do the opening. Now either push or pull the gate open so that it is wide enough to prevent it catching the horse's quarters or catching your knee. Keep the horse's head close to the latch end while you manoeuvre his quarters around until he's alongside the gate on the opposite side. Then lean over and fasten the gate.

In time your horse will become as adept as you are at opening gates and some will take a very active part, sidling up to the gate and then giving it a good push once you've unlatched it. This makes the whole thing a lot quicker and more amusing too.

Having made the whole operation sound so simple and straightforward, there are gates and gates, and not all are easy to open. Sometimes it is easier for both of you if you jump off and unhitch the gate from the ground, and safer too, even if it does mean that your boots sink into thick mud. A gate can be negotiated in 30 seconds by a well-trained horse and rider, but if you're fumbling about and making a mess of the whole thing it will take you very much longer.

If you are in front of other riders do make it clear whether you are going to hold the gate for them, or expect them to catch hold of the gate as they approach. Some gates swing shut rather abruptly and badly bruised knees can be the result. Also, beware of catching your martingale – or

There is a certain amount of roadwork to be found on competitive rides (Steve Moore)

your reins – in the gate, and never push it open with your foot, that's just asking for trouble.

Most rides will include some road-work so the long-distance horse does need to be traffic proof, bearing in mind that in competition fitness he is likely to be on his toes. Though he may normally ignore the most frightening lorry, he's likely to find any excuse to play up. Not all drivers slow down and some drivers may not even realise the dangers and will speed past obliviously, so it's up to you to take every possible precaution. If you see that a vehicle is approaching too fast, slow him down in advance. If there is a decent verge without drainage ditches, stick to that – but don't ride on pavements or ornamental grass verges.

Never fight your horse on a busy road: wait until the road is clear and then ride him past the obstacle, being very firm and determined. But if the traffic is continuous, dismount and lead him past. If you know that there is a busy road to tackle, try and ride with a school-master type and keep behind him. (You should only ride two abreast on wide, quiet roads.)

Stick to walk or trot where you can. Trotting downhill on a road is not a good idea, especially if the road is slippery, although trotting uphill is a good muscling-up exercise. Never canter on the road, the horse may get over-excited and the tarmac or concrete will jar his legs.

Always make your intentions clear when about to turn at a junction by giving the correct signals. Look over your shoulder to ensure that the traffic has acknowledged you before stopping or moving out into the road.

If turning right at crossroads, do not move to the centre of the road as you would if you were driving. Instead, keep to the left and when it is clear to cross, move in a straight line to take up position again on the left side of the road. On a roundabout you should keep to the left, even when turning right. Say thank you, or wave an acknowledgement to anyone who slows down for you; it could persuade the driver to do the same for the next horse he meets on the road.

DIFFERING NEEDS

Basically you should take your time and build up slowly to the longer, faster rides, taking care to put in all the necessary training and preparation. However, there is no point in over training. Always train for the competition ahead, and ride the same mileage and speed over the same type of terrain for that event, several times within a month of the competition. The last week should be an easy one, perhaps concentrating on any schooling problems – it is not the time to catch up in your training schedule, or introduce anything new.

PLEASURE & TRAINING RIDES

Any horse or rider can take part in these rides, usually without having to be a member of the group organising the ride. Usually a minimum speed of 5mph (8km) is given to ensure that riders do not dawdle along the route. There is no veterinary judging. Little preparation is needed at this level, and horses and ponies in regular work should be quite capable of completing pleasure ride distances without any problems. It is a good way of introducing young horses to the sport.

Maximum distance is 25 miles (40km). The horse should be accustomed to a training ride of six to ten miles, and you could increase this to 15 miles during the two weeks before the ride, lengthening your daily rides a little too. Your first competitive rides will be best used as a way of settling the horse to the sport.

Pleasure rides have no veterinary judging but there may be a tack inspection at the start of the ride, simply to check that your tack is safe and fits the horse correctly. So clean and check your saddle and bridle well in advance of the ride so that if you do find something which needs

PAGE 57: A vet examining a horse's mouth for lesions on the bars and corners of the mouth (Bob Langrish). (below) Liz Finney with Showgirl II and Roger Heeley with Sabre on what must have been one of the hottest Golden Horseshoe Rides in 1988 (Bob Langrish)
PAGES 58-9: A rider encourages her horse to drink at a stream. It is important, especially on a long ride, for a horse to drink where ever the opportunity presents itself (Bob Langrish)

repair you have time to take it to your saddler and have it mended. Do this anyway, for safety's sake.

Have your horse shod ten days or so before any ride, just to make sure that the shoes are bedded down enough and that the problems associated with new shoes – prick, sore feet, nail bind – will not cause trouble.

COMPETITIVE RIDES
· *TRIAL OR MEDAL RIDES* ·

Distances are from 20 to 60 miles (32 to 96km) and success in these rides is judged on speed and condition of the horse with time and veterinary parameters; a minimum speed is given for each category of ride. For instance, the BHS Bronze Buckle qualifier over 20 miles has a minimum speed of $6^{1}/_{2}$mph; the route may be completed at that speed or faster, and qualification also depends on whether the horse passes the veterinary inspection. Under EHPS rules there is a Novice CTR section of 20 or 25 miles (32 or 40km), ridden at speeds of 6 and 7mph.

On your first CTR rides it is wise to be content with low gradings and work your way up gradually. Otherwise you may suffer elimination at the beginning of your long distance riding career. Gradings are awarded according to the number of penalties incurred for speed or pulse rate. The age of your horse together with your own experience will dictate which rides you enter. An experienced rider with a riding club horse which is fairly fit, could start with longer pleasure rides, shorter distance CTRs, or Bronze Buckle qualifiers.

For a useful and long career your horse needs to have a good foundation of steady work and to be brought on gradually, season by season. The rider must be prepared to slow down if necessary, and alter goals according to the horse's reactions and progress.

In his first season use the pleasure rides and training rides to build up to 20 (32km) or 25 miles (40km). Never rush your horse in terms of the number of competitions or speed. The successful completion of a ride should be more highly prized than a trophy or medal. For a 25 mile (42km) ride your horse need only be hunting fit. When the next season starts he is likely to have retained a certain amount of fitness and should be quicker to bring up to ride fitness.

It is up to you and your horse whether you build up the distances in your second year, perhaps aiming for a 40 or 50 mile (64 or 80km) ride. Obviously, this will involve a planned training regime and a better

A contrast to the sense of hurried excitement as the rider takes a moment to concentrate on times and speed (Bob Langrish)

appreciation of the way your horse is going so that there is no risk of him suffering fatigue. Many successful riders work out a suitable training programme to fit in with a full-time job.

CTR, and Silver Stirrup rides are useful to work up to longer distance rides. In your third year you may be keen to go on to faster CTRs or endurance races.

ENDURANCE RIDES

These are race rides against the clock, where horses and riders compete against one another and the winner is the first across the finish line, *providing that* the horse is vetted sound. To compete in an EHPS endurance ride the rider must have proof of a grading in at least one ride of 40 miles.

Distances vary from 40 to 100 miles in one day, with vet gates along the route. Approached with care and preparation these can be very straight-forward. Dismount a mile from the gate and check the pulse rate with a stethoscope. Depending on the reading the rider may then remount and trot for half a mile and then walk, possibly leading the horse, the last half mile so that the horse is presented with a suitable pulse rate (64 or below). Tackled this way there is less chance of the horse being held up or eliminated. The vet gate will also include trotting up to check for signs of lameness, and checks for back sores, cuts or wounds. Look at the organising body's rules for full details, as they do vary.

Endurance rides have a massed start, with groups of varying size. However, if your horse is likely to become excited or uncontrollable, the organiser may allow you to start separately. On the first endurance ride the rider should aim to complete with a sound horse, and racing for a good position should be left to the more experienced.

In time the rider will develop tactics according to his own aims and the capabilities of his horse. Generally, it is better to ride with a small group and choose your own pace to suit horse and terrain rather than have it dictated at risk of tiring the horse too quickly.

CREW

Major rides, particularly where there are vet halts, call for a helper or crew. BHS rules demand a helper for all rides over 30 miles, although a rider who has achieved 'Gold Series' (Golden Horseshoe qualifier and Exmoor ride) status may do without a helper on Silver Stirrup qualifiers. The EHPS does not make any specific demands about helpers.

The crew must take charge of the horse should it be necessary and

If you can train your horse to walk or trot beside you, it will help you on a ride
(Bob Langrish)

provide a back-up service in an emergency. It may simply mean helping the rider to get organised at the start of the ride, meeting up at certain points on the route to see that all's well, supplying water and helping to make the horse comfortable at the end.

A good crew is invaluable to the rider and will make an important contribution to success. It is not an easy job. The helper must be able to read a map well, drive quickly to be at the right place at the right time, armed with whatever is needed for horse and rider. Other skills might include a thick skin and a sense of humour – tensions run high on a ride, particularly in the last few miles. Whatever the rider needs must be provided 'double quick' and heaven help the helper who cannot provide the requested article or has missed a scheduled meeting en route! You must be able to work as a team and your teamwork must come together before the ride.

When you receive the ride details go over them together so that you can decide where the horse should drink – this will take into consideration difficult going, and where there are streams. These meeting points must be easily accessible for the helper's vehicle and not be so isolated that it is difficult to get to the next stop on time.

The helper must have a copy of the relevant Ordnance Survey map with the ride route etched onto it and the times that the rider expects to reach certain checkpoints. A whole host of items should be packed into the back-up vehicle so that they are easily accessible and recognisable by coloured bags or large print labels.

Water is the most important, and it is wise to take a minimum of two water carriers and two or three buckets; it makes life easier if one of the carriers has electrolytes ready mixed in. Remember sponges, invaluable for cooling the horse off, and drinks for the rider, too.

Tack spares should include a bridle, reins, stirrup leathers, girth, girth sleeve (if used) and numnah. For halts there should be a cooler rug, headcollar and lead rope, grooming kit – which must include a hoof pick and sweatscraper – and stethoscope.

First-aid kits for the horse should contain wound powder, Animalintex, bandages, scissors; neat electrolytes, a spare set of shoes and fly repellent. The rider's kit should contain all the usual; plasters, liniment and bandages, headache and stomach pills. Take a spare pair of jodhpurs, boots jacket and gloves for the rider to ensure against the weather and accidents.

At the halts the helper will need to work quickly, making the horse comfortable and helping to cool him off especially if it is a hot day. For

Candy Cameron, Scottish Champion, with White Trooper. Note the covered stirrup iron which permits her, under ride rules, to wear running shoes (Bob Langrish)

the vetting, the helper should be wearing the same competitor number as the rider. If the horse trots up sound, it's back to the vehicle to tack up again using the fresh numnah and girth. Then pack up and tear off to the next arranged meeting spot.

If the ride is on a hot day the helper will be welcomed at as many points as possible on the route with wet sponges to cool the horse, water for the horse and refreshment for the rider. Fill large squash bottles with water and hand them, screw-top removed, to the rider to pour over the horse (and perhaps himself!)

By the finish the rider may a little more fraught. The helper must stay calm and follow the same procedure quickly but quietly so as not to fluster either horse or rider.

On major rides the helper should accompany the rider to the pre-ride briefings and make a note of any alterations to the route, tricky sections etc, to remind the rider if necessary. Note also the position of vets and blacksmiths, and any emergency telephone numbers.

· RIDER EQUIPMENT & CLOTHING ·

BHS and EHPS rules state that a rider must wear a jockey skull BSI 4472 or riding hat BSI 6473. Most riders use the lightweight brands of jockey skulls. They may wear whatever type of riding boot they prefer - long leather or rubber riding boots or jodhpur boots. On longer or difficult rides when a rider anticipates walking with the horse or if it is likely to be hot, short walking boots are usually preferable. Footwear with a heel of less than half an inch may only be worn if a caged or otherwise adapted stirrup iron is used to prevent the foot from slipping through.

Spurs are not allowed but a whip is permitted, providing it is not more than 30 inches (76.2cm) in length. As far as other clothing goes, the key word is the same as that for the horse's tack – comfort. A seam in the wrong place might rub, and avoid anything which is too tight, or too thick and warm. Don't forget that all that activity is likely to make you hot and uncomfortable. Cotton-type sweatshirt tops are ideal; cotton-mix jodhpurs are more comfortable on a long day than nylon. Your jacket must be water-proof but made of material which will breathe such as waxed cotton. Water-proof over-trousers are a good idea too providing your horse does not object to any 'rustling' sound they might make – scrunched up small they can be carried in your pocket or saddlebag. A quilted waistcoat is comfortable for rides since it is not too bulky, and leaves your arms free. When it's cold it is best to dress in layers so that if you do warm up you can discard a jumper or waistcoat in the direction of your helper. Stick to natural fibres which will absorb perspiration.

5 Getting Started

Any horse has it in him to take part on long distance rides – any breed, type, age or sex. You can only assess whether you or he are suited to it when you actually get out and have a go. See if your horse can cope with what you are asking, and if you both enjoy it; start at the bottom – and start with the horse or pony you already have, whatever it is. Some have turned their talents to long distancing at the ripe old age of 25! Go along to a pleasure ride or a local group's social ride, talk to other riders and see whether you really are interested.

You might decide to stick to 15 and 25 mile rides (24 to 40km) for your first season. For many, 25 miles is a quite acceptable limit for a long distance. The following season you may start with another pleasure ride, and then have a go at a Novice Competitive Trail Ride (CTR), or a Bronze Buckle ride, which will demand a faster pace and have veterinary inspections before and after the ride.

By now you should know how far you want to pursue your new-found sport and how suitable your mount is – perhaps due to conformational faults it has begun to injure itself, by brushing for example; its feet may be too prone to bruising or as a result of the different feeding and exercise programme the horse may be less manageable, so that handling him on rides is difficult. Perhaps he 'switches off' and is difficult to keep going, which is just as hard work. If you are 'hooked' you might want to change your mount for something more ambitious.

Don't get into a panic about your first ride. You might worry about having a minimum speed, and pacing yourself. But there really is nothing to it. Why not arrange to ride with someone with experience who will be willing to 'show you the ropes'?

Most horses or ponies can cope with a pleasure ride without any real preparation, though it will take that initial bit of competition to reveal their true level of fitness.

TRAINING

How much you train and the methods you use will depend on a number of things:
1 Your horse: his age, experience and type;
2 Your area: whether flat or hilly, town or country and the facilities available to you;
3 The level of fitness you are aiming at;
4 The amount of time you have available.

(left) A considerate rider makes things easier for her horse by lightening his load and leading him down a steep escarpment (Bob Langrish)

If a horse is pushed too hard the risk of breakdown is increased, and the experience of pain may sour him and could certainly limit his career. We can strive for a goal in our training and put up with pain and discomfort, but the horse knows no such rationalised ambitions and can only obey his rider to the best of his ability.

Young horses are more susceptible to stress and, particularly if they are physically immature, will be unable to cope with the demands made of them. They require more regular exercise than an older horse to maintain fitness. If your horse is naturally keen he will be easy to get fit but difficult to contain when excited whereas a calm horse may take longer but will retain a placid temperament.

A training programme should revolve around three things: specificity – that is, training for what is required (short bursts of fast exercise would obviously not get a horse fit enough for a 100-mile ride; individualism; and commonsense.

Select the training method that suits you, your horse and your environment. Once again it comes down to the fact that the horse is an individual and needs to be treated accordingly; he is not a machine that you can programme to do what you require. It is unwise to pick a training regime and follow it word for word, it may not altogether suit your horse's individuality. Be flexible and watch your horse carefully. Keep an eye on his mental attitude, his feeding habits and so on, and tailor your own training programme to his particular needs.

Commonsense is important: if your horse is undergoing periods of overstress which may lead to minor problems, you must make the appropriate alteration to the training programme and/or feeding. Over-feeding and making a horse too fit can cause many problems, particularly for the inexperienced rider.

The rider should be looking to improve the horse's energy production to withstand fatigue, and trying to build up psychological familiarity so that the horse will participate in competitions in a relaxed manner, conserving energy. Three things need to be achieved in a successful training programme: suppleness and strength, and stamina, the latter being the most important for the long distance horse. Training will condition the body in the following ways:

1 The muscular system will be improved to give greater capacity for energy production.
2 The cardiovascular system will be improved, with an increase in the size of the heart, in the capillary supply to the muscle and blood volume.
3 Though the lungs are unlikely to be enlarged or altered, some

improvement in gas transfer may occur as well as in adaptation of the respiratory muscles.

4 In the nervous system there may be better integration for improved co-ordination, and faster firing of nerves.

5 Thermo-regulation: this is conditioning the horse to be able to cope with heat.

Training should produce similar stresses to those expected in competition. If you use your horse to only half the capacity that he is expected to produce on the day, you cannot then expect him to perform perfectly. Fifty per cent of the fibres within a particular muscle will have been worked in training, where 100 per cent may be needed in competition. Obviously, the 50 per cent that were not previously used cannot be expected to function as well as those which have been trained, and so they rapidly become fatigued. Appreciation of this aspect of training will help to reduce the risk of injury and improve performance.

Although we have become used to stress as something which is bad for us, it is actually a necessary part of our lives. For the horse, used in the right way, it has the beneficial effect of building up the body's systems to cope with the new demands. What happens is this: the body is given an external stimulus which it is not used to, and changes to adapt to it. Through the extra demands made in exercise the body undergoes various alterations, including those within the muscles, so that it can better tolerate the next challenge.

This process may not always take place without the horse undergoing some problems. If the stress were too great the horse might suffer tendon sprains, fractures, or at the extreme, death. It should therefore be used gradually, increasing the workload and allowing sufficient recovery periods.

One cannot ask indefinitely of the horse. Each individual has a stress threshold and there will come a time in his training when he reaches a peak and cannot be taken any further. When overstressed the horse is more susceptible to viral infections because the immune system becomes particularly depressed.

· PULSE, RESPIRATION AND TEMPERATURE ·

These three provide vital information for the long distance rider: they will be referred to in training, since competition rules include minimum rates of pulse and respiration, and are used to govern the grade given on completion of a ride.

The average normal pulse is between 36 and 42 beats, and respiration is 8 to 16 breaths per minute; normal temperature is 100–101°F. Any change in condition of the horse can be monitored via the corresponding change in these rates.

The basic training programme should be made up of three types of exercise. Firstly, low intensity exercise of moderate duration – this will improve suppleness and joint mobility, and if the horse has had complete rest, will allow him to become re-accustomed to the saddle and the rider's weight. The second stage will have the horse working harder, developing his muscles, heart and circulation. Then, having reached the level of fitness appropriate to the rider's level of competition, the horse will progress to the third stage – maintenance exercise, which should keep him at his peak.

'Slow and steady' must identify the horse's initial training. A long period of slow conditioning will promote stamina, that essential 'staying power' which is the foundation for the more arduous work you will present your horse with as his training progresses. So, do not shirk on the walking and light trotting exercise. Some people spend up to a month on walking exercise alone if the horse has had a winter break, starting with half-an-hour a day and building up to three hours. This strengthens the leg muscles, tendons and ligaments, helps improve the mobility of joints, and encourages the tissues to adapt to what is being asked of them.

Trotting work can be increased as condition is built up – the horse by now should have lost any excess weight. These slow stages should last for at least a month. Canter work is introduced only when stamina and muscle strength are well developed. If early work is not done gradually and thoroughly there is a greater risk of the horse becoming lame.

Throughout the training procedure the horse's whole body system is conditioned and 'built up' – the heart, lungs, muscles and skeleton, until the tissues reach a pitch just below injury. This is known as *stress*. The body responds by strengthening the various parts as more is asked of them.

The second stage of training is when real fitness is developed, and the rider must start to tune the horse into the task ahead of it. For endurance rides the horse needs to increase his aerobic capacity and thus raise the anaerobic threshold. Either continuous or intermittent exercise schedules can be followed.

The 'continuous' form of training concentrates on covering the distance at slower speeds, the duration and intensity increased to correspond with the level of competition being aimed at. In the final two weeks before a ride, training should include one long ride just under the distance of the competition distance, and the overall intensity of work should be decreased.

Endurance horses will benefit from high-intensity work-outs in their training because these will improve their capacity to maintain high speeds

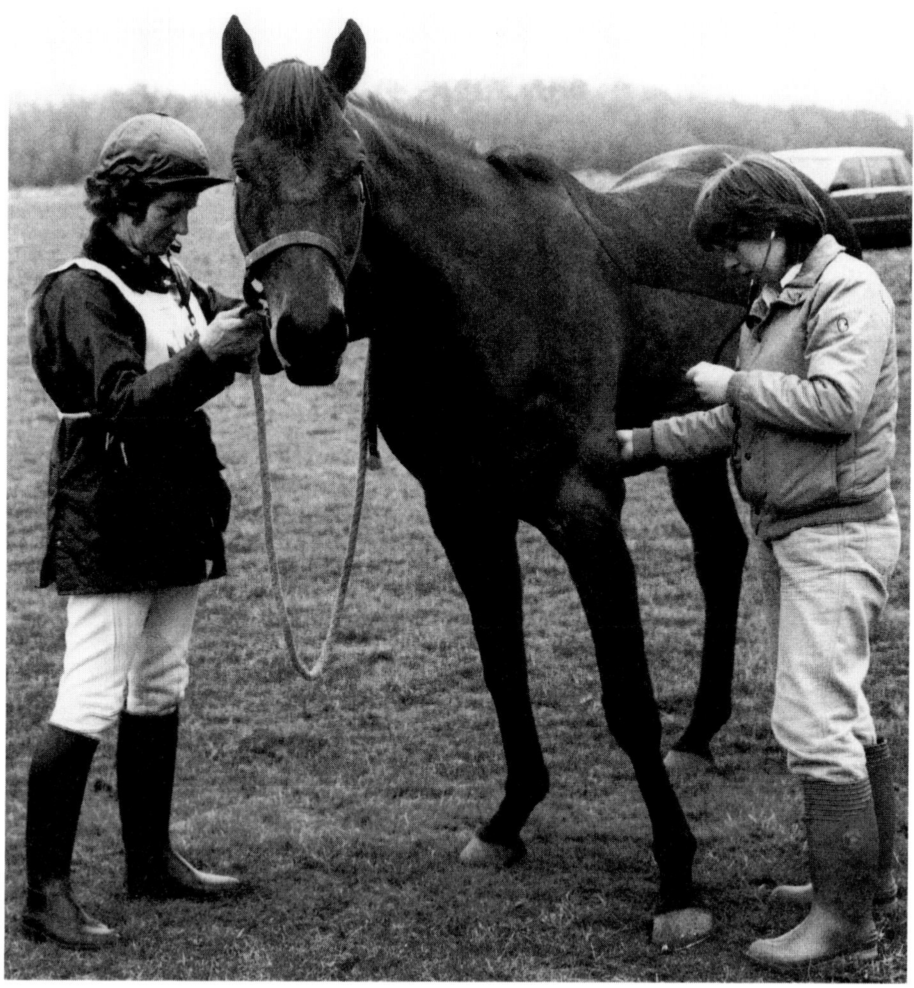

A veterinary assistant takes the pulse, using a stethoscope and watch, prior to the start of the ride (Steve Moore)

and to cope with ascending steep hills. This is where interval training has much to offer.

· INTERVAL TRAINING ·

Interval training is a method by which you can give the horse more intense work than if he was worked in one continuous period. He will be given a period of specific work (say, up to 10 mins), followed by an interval of semi-rest (also approximately 10 mins), then asked to work again (for up to 10 mins). The second period of work begins before the horse has had a chance to fully recover from the first. By exposing the body to *limited* amounts of stress alternated with rest, the respiratory and circulation rates are improved with minimum risk of physical damage.

It is essential that before starting an interval training programme the horse has a good foundation of long, slow work. Once you set out on your programme there is obviously a lot of room for variation in the duration and frequency of repetitions, but when the horse first starts, the work interval should be less intense and the repetitions fewer.

This system helps to increase stamina so that the horse can maintain a certain speed for a longer distance. The aim is to develop more resistance to fatigue by increasing the efficiency of the respiratory and cardio-vascular systems. This is accomplished by stressing the muscular system then allowing partial recovery during an interval of walking, then repeating the stress section. Though a more time-consuming process, the results of training will be better. The improved aerobic capacity is ideal for endurance races.

Interval training must be combined with regular monitoring of the reaction by the heart, lungs and body temperature. The shorthand for this is TPR – temperature, pulse, respiration. The reading of these is vital, and will give you a positive guide to the horse's state of fitness or health.

The horse's normal temperature is 38°C (100°F). It can vary by a degree either way, depending on the age of the horse and time of day, but a higher or lower temperature will indicate stress of some kind, or illness. Use a clean rectal thermometer, greased with petroleum jelly (Vaseline for example), and place it full-length into the rectum for one to two minutes to achieve a reading.

Normal pulse rate, at rest is 32–44 per minute. To take the horse's pulse, either place your fingers under the jawbone and feel the horse's facial artery, or use a stethoscope just below the elbow on the left side. Count the beats for 15 seconds, then multiply by four to calculate the heart rate per minute.

The normal respiration rate is 8 to 16 per minute. To make a count, watch the horse's flank and count only the inhalations, again for 15 seconds then multiply by four, for a minute's count. Or, put your hand over the horse's nostrils and count the number of exhalations.

To establish your horse's normal rates, do your TPR checks when he is at rest and calm. The rates you acquire after exercise can then be compared with the resting rates. Neither pulse nor respiration should be allowed to exceed the safety limit of 100 during work.

When you start interval training use only two repetitions of your work (stress) and rest intervals. This should not over-stress the horse, though if it does you should reduce the work period, the pace, or change your work area for easier terrain. Work, or stress, should be built up gradually, by repeating the sets of intervals. There should be no more than five intervals.

· WALKING ·

Walking is essential as a warming up and cooling off exercise. At the start of the ride it will help blood circulation throughout the body, in preparation for the stress of the faster work to come. It will also give the rider a chance to detect any lameness. After exercise, walking helps the horse to recover, and the blood circulation is decreased slowly, which helps remove lactic acid from the muscles and bloodstream.

Hill work has several advantages as it helps to build up certain muscle groups in the front and back legs. Also, the same physical effort can be maintained at a slower speed up hill than it can over flat ground.

If all this sounds like hard work, to be done by those with plenty of time on their hands, you'd be wrong. The majority of British competitors combine their horses with jobs, homes and families. It is possible to achieve fitness by riding only every other day providing longer rides are given at weekends, and as long as the horse can exercise himself in a field on a daily basis. A horse will maintain peak condition longer if he is brought up slowly, and the drop-off is more gradual.

FITNESS IN THE LONG DISTANCE HORSE

The essential aim of long distance riding is to have the horse fit enough for the work expected of it and to have it finish in good condition with minimum risk of either injury or fatigue. A definition of fitness is for the horse to be well adapted for a particular purpose, in good athletic condition and of good health. It is about tuning up its body systems so that they can give an adequate response to the task set by the rider, and to the ride it is competing in. Obviously, to compete effectively a horse will need to be ridden on long distances as part of his training.

Long distance and endurance riding can cause severe distress in a horse that has not been properly prepared, so a careful and unhurried training programme of regular work is essential. There really are no short cuts to fitness.

Correct feeding and good stable management must go hand in hand with fitness training. The rider must be observant of the horse's mental and physical state of health, and be ready to respond to any changes.

Generally, fitness should be attained by a steady increase in the work load together with an increase in the nutritional level of feeding to meet the horse's new requirements.

· *FITNESS LEVEL* ·

One of the best methods to assess any improvement is to time the horse working over a set distance and to monitor his speed as his training progresses.

The level of fitness the horse can achieve will depend very much on his inherent ability. This includes genetic factors such as constitution, and is also affected by the diet and method of training. All these will decide whether the horse can achieve the limit of his own ability. In fact, the real proof of the level of fitness can only be judged on the day of the competition.

One of the problems with training is that it is difficult to judge exactly when the desired stage of fitness has been achieved, but this may come with experience. You will learn to read the signs, for instance a change in the horse's gait will indicate the start of fatigue.

The respiratory rate is also an indication of the horse's state of fitness. In some countries this is one of the criteria for assessing whether a horse should be allowed to continue after the mandatory halts in an endurance ride. Deep and frequent respiration can be an indication of fatigue and will usually be accompanied by a high heart rate. In Britain if the respiratory rate reaches twice the heart rate after a 30 minute halt the horse is eliminated.

However, it has been argued that respiratory rates should not be used in this way as they may not necessarily indicate a fatigued horse. In America and Australia the respiratory rates are noted but high rates do not result in elimination. Increased respiratory rates can occur in a horse which pants as a means of cooling down. This can be seen on rides in hot conditions when horses take quick shallow breaths.

Weight will also be a guide; after all, you are aiming to turn fatness into fitness. It is as well to know your horse's weight, to assess his level of fitness and to help you with feeding him. The best and most accurate way to check your horse's weight is to take him to a local weighbridge. Every horse has his own optimum weight for performance. The more weight that is carried, the more energy is needed to carry the horse across the ground. It is true that fat is a source of energy for the horse and even the leanest horse still has sufficient stores of fat to utilise.

USING YOUR LOCAL AREA FOR TRAINING

Ideally, your horse should be ridden over a variety of terrain to prepare him for whatever he might encounter when you start taking him to organised rides. Finding new routes will also prevent him from becoming bored.

Obviously, the type of terrain you can train on depends very much where you live and what access you have to the local countryside. Hills are not necessary for getting a horse fit providing that adequate time and distance are put into training, though they are useful for building up muscle.

Opinions differ on the usefulness of road work in 'hardening up' the legs. The horse will suffer strain and concussion if trotted hard and fast on roads without any preparation. If you are forced to do much road work do plenty of walking before you move on to trot work.

Use the grass verge to save your horse's legs and shoes, but don't be tempted to canter unless the road is very quiet and you know it well. In Britain, the number of road accidents involving horses is unbelievably high and if your horse spooks at something in the hedge he may end up in the path of a car. Also, beware of drainage ruts where your horse could catch a hind leg.

Try to introduce your horse to the 'obstacles' that he is likely to meet when competing. For a youngster this could include the most obvious things such as streams. Buy a large-scale map of your area as this will help you work out new ride routes using bridleways, and will develop your map-reading skills.

More and more riders are valuing bridleways, particularly as roads get busier, and local authorities are gradually waking up to the need for maintaining them, and are even creating new ones. The BHS, the regional representatives of the Bridleways Association, and the Countryside Commission have had a great part to play in this. Over the years many bridleways have become blocked or removed, but riders seem to have become more willing to take action when they find obstructions such as locked gates; the matter can be taken up by a local representative of the authorities mentioned.

Before you set out on any exploration, check with your county BHS bridleways officer or your local bridleway society that the route is accessible. They may also be able to tell you of any new routes. Some areas are much better served than others – the Cotswolds, for instance, has a good network of bridleways, and in South Yorkshire the county council has half-a-dozen or so route cards detailing a selection of bridleways throughout the county.

If you have a problem and want to tackle it yourself, go to your district council office and ask to see the definitive map of the area. Make a note of the official number given to the pathway in question, and any others linked with it, and then ask to see the Rights of Way Officer; explain the problem and ask him to take action. Keep in touch until the problem has been resolved.

If the path is not marked on the map as a bridleway but has been used as one for many years, ask the council for a supply of 'Public Rights of Way Evidence' forms. If a certain number of people complete these, and thereby prove that a path has been used as a bridleway for a sufficient number of years, then it may be upgraded to bridlepath status.

More long distance bridleways are likely to be created in this country, and one day riders may even be able to ride around the country via linking bridleways. Those currently in existence include Peddar's Way in Norfolk (from King's Lynn to Thetford), Swan's Way (from Goring-on-Thames to Salcey Forest in Northamptonshire), South Downs Way, the Ridgeway and North Downs Way.

You must stick to the 'country code': close gates behind you, treat other people using the pathway with respect, ride slowly past livestock and keep to the bridleway. It is worth avoiding bridleways in the winter when they are muddy, so that they don't turn into impassable quagmires.

Riders have the legal right to ride on all public highways except footpaths and motorways. Here are a few more rights concerning bridleways.

1 The highway authority is required by law to erect a signpost at every point where a bridleway or byway joins a metalled road, unless they agree with the parish council that this is not necessary.
2 It is an offence to put up any sign or notice containing false or misleading information that is likely to deter people from using a public right of way along a bridleway or byway, provided the right of way is shown on the definitive map.
3 The Countryside Commission has a code of practice on the ploughing of public paths which advises farmers of their duties in respect of ploughing and planting crops on public rights of way.
4 If you find a highway obstructed you may remove just enough of the obstruction so you can pass, with the minimum of damage; if the way has been blocked by the landowner or occupier, you should politely but firmly continue to exercise your rights. A more practical course is to ride around any obstruction, taking care not to cause damage.

The Forestry Commission encourages sensible riders to enjoy their woodlands, but before you can do so you must obtain a permit; this costs around £15 and you may have to carry an identity tag. Riders must stick to the allotted routes. A lot of National Trust land is private, but riders have access via bridleways, and can ride over their moorland, fell and common land.

Disused railway lines sometimes provide good long rides. They usually have a reasonable surface (*some can be stony*) and are often well away from the noise and peril of roads. But watch out for rabbit-holes! You may also be allowed to ride in your local country

Map reading is one of the most important skills to master for success in the sport.
A momentary glance at your map could save you heading off in the wrong direction
(Bob Langrish)

park, keeping to marked paths – ask the park warden or district council for details.

Interval training requires a certain amount of measured space. If you can't use your own field, why not ask your local riding school if you could use a schooling paddock a couple of times a week? You may have to make a small payment but it is sure to be worth it. Alternatively, why not ask neighbouring farmers if they have an area suitable?

Riding on a beach can be a smashing way of giving your horse some fast work, particularly during the winter months, even if you have to drive for an hour or so to get there. But check with the local council that they allow horses on the beach and sort out where you can leave your horsebox. Also, check the tides before you set out, you don't want to be caught by the rising tide. A tide timetable can be obtained from the local marina or newsagent.

MAP READING

It is essential that you have the right type of map and know how to use it. On a ride markers may get moved, or knocked flat and out of sight. You must be able to check quickly with your map, pick out your position (perhaps by also using a compass), and take up the correct route. So become familiar with maps and the valuable information they hold.

Start by going to your newsagent or bookshop and buying yourself the Ordnance Survey map of the area around your home, an OS 1:50000 series map which has a bright pink cover.

Take a good look at the key and the symbols for bridleways and byways (you can ride these too), and also footpaths, which you must not ride on. Get used to working out where you are and where you are going. Take your map for a walk, converting what is on the map to what you see around you. Begin by following footpaths or bridleways which are familiar to you, always referring to your map as you go. That way you can check your map interpretation because you should know exactly where you are.

Before starting to walk, set the map by pointing the top edge towards the north. Get your bearings by looking for two or three features in the distance, ie houses, woodland, bridges. Check that the direction in which they lie tallies with the direction shown on the map. If it does not, rotate the map until it does. Then off you go.

You will need to recognise hills and valleys, streams and woodlands from your map. Both hills and valleys are indicated by brown contour lines and can be confused – (just remember that streams normally belong in valleys.) These lines are marked in vertical intervals and join together at equal height, which is usually marked alongside each line. The closer the lines are together, the steeper the hill or valley. On higher ground there are often spot heights, a series of numbers indicating the height above sea level, in the centre of the lines. In time, you will find that a quick glance at the map will instantly give you a picture of the lie of the land.

Flat land can be recognised on the map by the absence of contour lines – in hilly country this may represent the floor of a valley or plateau. A straight slope is represented by lines which are spread evenly over a distance. A concave slope (curving inwards) can be recognised by a distinct progressive increase in the spread of the contour lines from those in close proximity on high land to the more spread out on lower land. Convex slopes (curving outwards) can be identified by a distinct progressive increase in the spread of contour lines from those in close proximity at a low level to those more spread out on high land.

Undulating land is shown on the map as a series of contour lines of only two or three different heights, but fairly close to one another. An escarpment is a steep slope, indicated by the contour lines being drawn closer together. Hill tops may be shown as conical hills where contour lines resemble a bull's eye.

Your next step is probably to plan a circular bridleway route to try out on horseback. Be a bit more adventurous and try an area you don't normally hack over. At this stage the OS 1:25000 series map might be more useful as it is one mile (1.6km) to $2^1/_2$in (6.25cm), and is therefore easier to read. The light blue cover maps have been updated by the green ones which differentiate between footpaths and bridleways. If you can only find the light blue map mark in the bridleways in ink from your OS 1:50000 map.

The 1:25000 map is large enough to show fields and is very easy to read, though you may find yourself having to turn and re-fold the map more often. Not an easy thing to do on horseback – you might find yourself travelling further and faster than you had intended! So it's probably better to hop off for a good look at your map.

Make sure your planned circular route is no longer than you can comfortably manage. To do this, cut yourself a short length of string and lay it on the map over the route you intend to take. Then measure the length of string taken up by the route, and translate it into miles as follows: on a 1:25000 series map (larger scale) each $2^1/_2$in (6.25cm) represents one mile; on a 1:50000 series map (smaller scale) each $1^1/_4$in (2.75cm) of string represents one mile (1.6km). Allow yourself a little extra mileage if the route is hilly.

Give yourself plenty of time. Preferably set out in the morning and tell someone back at home where you are heading. Keep a coin for the phone in your pocket, together with a slip of paper with your name and address on it in case you fall off and are knocked unconscious. Attach a dog tag with your name, address and phone number to the saddle.

Start training yourself to be observant. Before you set off, study the map well and try to note a few landmarks, ie bridges or churches, which might help you remember the turns, left or right, you have to make. Map reading can be difficult, especially in a strange area. For instance, if you're not travelling north, in the direction that your map is drawn, you could quite easily find yourself turning right when you should have turned left. And when riding across moorland it can feel more like navigating across the sea.

By the time you enter your first pleasure ride you should feel a little more confident about it all. The secretary will send you a route map which is likely to be a photocopy of an OS map with the route for your class marked out in a thick pen. Since the photocopy will be in black and white you will find it difficult to identify the types of roads, so buy yourself the map of the area and copy the route sent you onto your Ordnance Survey map using a soft pencil. To make reading the photocopy easier, many riders also find it useful to colour in the roads (red, A road; orange, B road; etc).

Your ride organiser should use a grid reference to indicate where the ride starts and finishes. Ordnance Survey maps are divided into squares of vertical and horizontal lines. Each line is given a number which is marked at the top and bottom edges of the map, and on either side. In a grid reference the first three numbers refer to the vertical lines, and the second three to the horizontal lines.

Ideally, you should also drive to the area and have a look around, perhaps walk some of the route. That way it won't be so strange on the day and you won't be quite so nervous.

It is a good idea to be able to use a compass in conjunction with your map reading. It is particularly useful when you start riding longer distances and tackling the moorland rides where, if you do get lost, you may find it difficult to discover exactly where you are just by looking at the map. Thick cloud could come down and leave you riding almost blindly on.

Here's how to use your compass. Suppose you are by a cairn and you want to head towards a stream. Place your compass alongside the cairn on the map. Turn the dial so that the orienting lines on the transparent bottom are parallel with grid lines running north to south on the map, the arrow pointing north. Then turn the whole compass, plus map, until the red end of the magnetic needle points north. Look up and distinguish a rock or other landmark that lies along the line shown by the travel arrow. Ride towards it, then look up another landmark in the same way, and so on.

Maps and compasses need to be looked at quickly so they must be readily available for you to check at a glance. The answer is a clear folder (available cheaply at large stationers' or outdoor pursuits' shops) attached by cord around the rider's neck and arm. Alternatively, there are dual-purpose bibs or tabards which incorporate clear pockets below the competitor number to take the map and compass. On rides which are well marked or familiar you could probably manage with a map folded in your jacket pocket.

COPING WITH TERRAIN

The horse should be ridden over a variety of terrain to prepare him for when he starts competing. So there is a very good case for loading him into your horsebox and taking him to different areas to exercise. This in itself could be a good preparation for what is to come, and will prevent him from becoming bored. And a happy, interested horse is more resistant to fatigue.

Horse and rider should know how to tackle hills, and the horse particularly must find the most economical way of going up and down. Finding steep hills in a Welsh competition ride might come as a bit of a shock to the horse if he has only been used to gentle slopes.

Although riding uphill makes greater demands on the horse's energy, it is physically easier for him than going down, since his power comes from his hind legs. To help him the rider must keep his weight close to the horse's centre of gravity – the degree to which your body must fold depends on the steepness of the hill. Keep your back straight, keep your head up and look forward, maintaining your leg position. Allow the horse to take as much extra rein as he needs, keeping a light contact. Keep your legs on to maintain impulsion but don't niggle the horse. On a very steep hill you might find it easier to ride in a zig-zag.

With a steep descent, it is important that the rider keeps the horse straight; if the quarters swing too far out of line the horse may lose his balance, slide sideways or even fall. Sit still and straight, taking care not to tilt to one side. Keep him going forwards with a light contact on the reins to keep him steady. Some horses prefer to go downhill with their noses to the ground. If this is the case then you must just let him get on with it and ignore the fact that you have nothing in front of you!

Many riders prefer to dismount and walk or jog beside the horse to go down hills. Trotting downhill is often easier for the horse, providing it is not too steep and the same principles of balance and straightness apply. You should rise to the trot, or semi-stand in the stirrups without bumping in the saddle.

It is quite possible to canter and gallop downhill, given the right going and gradient. Have your horse in a balanced canter and in control before you start descending. You will have trouble altering the pace or your state of control once you are on the hill. The horse will lengthen his stride and naturally increase speed, but this is less likely to get out of hand if he began on a short, bouncy canter.

Don't try to control the pace by hanging on to the reins, it will cause the horse to hollow his back and lose his back end and balance, so he will go faster still. Instead, use your legs and body, and a sensitive rein contact, to keep the horse in his rounded shape. The horse may break into a gallop down a slope because he has not been ridden well enough in canter or because the gradient is too steep for him to be able to keep his balance. If he does there is very little you can do, and it is quite likely that you will reach the bottom out of control. Adopt a position over the centre of motion, further back than you would on the flat and keep your lower leg a little in front of the girth. Keep the horse on the bit with a rein contact that will allow him to adopt the head carriage that he prefers.

You may occasionally find yourself riding across a slope. This is not so easy for the horse as he constantly has to re-adjust his balance to stay upright. Sit still and square in the saddle, keeping your 'downhill' leg firmly on the girth. Stick to your pace.

· RIVERS AND STREAMS ·

Most mature horses will go through water with little problem. If you are in a bunch with other horses don't follow too closely because if the rider in front has problems and topples off you could risk trampling on him; or if *your* horse is forced to take evasive action, you may find yourself in the water. River beds, particularly in upland areas, are often strewn with loose, weed-encrusted boulders, giving an insecure footing. The stones may rock when stepped on and frighten the horse, particularly if he is young and inexperienced. He may freeze, or plunge to one side, but stay calm and keep still in the saddle, allow him the rein he needs, and urge him positively across the stream, with legs and voice.

· BAD GOING ·

It is important to know how to cope with bad going and the rider should always respond sensitively to the horse's efforts and remain balanced.

Some horses don't seem to be affected by hard ground. Others, with thin soles or conformational faults which accentuate jarring, hate it. Any horse may be badly affected by prolonged work at faster gaits on a hard surface, and joints and tendons especially are put under great strain. Particularly bad are hard, rutted areas, a hard beaten path and chalk uplands in the summer which can become as hard as rock. A horse 'feeling' hard ground will shorten his stride and move with less zest than usual.

Moorland areas feature rocky outcrops which in fact will cause little damage to the horse, unlike flints. But a horse can still jar or bruise himself, and the rider should be alert to any signs of the horse going short. It could be a knock causing momentary pain, but if lameness is marked or persists, you must dismount and investigate.

· *SLIPPERY GROUND AND MUD* ·

Slippery surfaces include a thin layer of wet soil over rock or gravel, or where the top few millimetres of chalk have been softened by rain; loose scree on slopes, moss-covered boulders and some types of mud. The worst is frost and ice which you may possibly encounter on your early morning training rides. The best advice is to use commonsense and take care.

Moving through heavy, sticky ground is tiring for the horse, and when he is unfit or tired there is a risk of tendon strain. Some horses can handle mud and manage to keep their rhythm, others really get bogged down by it. The rider can help in all cases by sitting quietly, and retaining a light rein contact with the legs firmly on to keep the horse moving straight and forwards.

· *BOGS* ·

Obviously you must try to avoid bogs, so keep your eyes peeled and follow the route given to you, especially in the New Forest, Dartmoor, Exmoor and similar areas in Wales and Scotland.

If you find your horse sinking fetlock deep in sucking, smelly going, retrace your steps straight away, and head for higher, firmer ground. Boggy areas can generally be identified by sharply contrasting colours, a brighter growth amongst drier fern and heather. Many horses have a sixth sense to detect bogs and other hazards, so pay attention to your mount – if you feel that your horse is slowing up or quickening against your wishes, you must be sensitive to the possible causes.

TIMINGS AND PACINGS

The long distance rider must learn to judge the optimum speed of his horse and adjust the pace to the terrain and to meet the timings required in competition. You will need to know the horse's speeds at walk, trot and canter. The first two can be done on the road – work out a distance from a mile to ten miles, then ride it in either pace; use your map to work out a distance on a bridleway or suitable open space to time the horse in canter.

You should aim to build up the speed in trot, a key gait in long distance riding – some horses are able to travel faster in trot than in canter. Work out different distances (10 miles, 8 miles) on your training rides and practise your timing, setting yourself speeds to aim for, 10mph, 8mph and so on. Encourage your horse to work in a good rhythm, in his best pace. Once he learns to settle into it, it will be less tiring and more economical on a ride.

A lot of time can be lost negotiating hills, and the rider must learn to work on an average mph. If working to a speed of 8mph for example, the hills may reduce your speed to 5mph, so when the going is better you will have to go at a faster pace to make up time, so as to average out at the optimum speed.

The speed specified for a competitive trail or medal ride sets an optimum time (for the ride to be completed in): Bronze Buckle rides need to be run at $6^{1}/_{2}$mph which would take roughly 3 hours, 5 minutes (the time required to complete). CTRs, under EHPS rules, require a speed of between 7 and 8mph – on a 25-mile ride a speed of 8mph would take 3 hours, 7 minutes and 30 seconds.

The skill comes in interpreting what is on the map and working out roughly the speed that you will be able to cover that particular ground in. Hilly, difficult terrain, roads and stony tracks will demand a slower speed, whereas good going across open moorland or good bridleways will allow a faster pace and the chance to make up time.

Your competitor's notes should tell you how many checkpoints there are on your ride, and their distance apart. Work out the speed that you want to aim for in each section, then the time it should take you to reach each one. When you have your start time, work it out exactly from that. You could set your watch at 12 o'clock when you start, an easy way of keeping track of the hours and minutes as they pass.

Work out your times using a calculator. For instance, if you wanted to work at 8mph, divide 8 into 60, then multiply the resulting figure by the number of miles you are doing.

Note each time down and keep it either on your map or somewhere where you can easily see it – Biro scribbled on the back of the hand is a method used by many, but watch it doesn't rub off! Pass the checkpoint timings on to your helper too, if he or she is planning to meet you en route.

6 Feeding

Feeding is a fairly daunting subject which demands thought and knowledge. Many owners find it quite a task to work out a diet which will provide all that the horse requires, including energy, without the horse becoming too 'hot'. The process may involve a certain amount of experimentation, with advice from feed experts and fellow riders.

The nutrition of the horse is an inaccurate science, besides which every horse is an individual. The specific food type and the amounts that he can cope with are determined by his particular make-up and 'medical' history. For instance, if he suffered worm damage as a youngster his metabolism will have altered accordingly.

It is sometimes argued that nature should be left to its own devices, particularly when talking about supplements. But it should be remembered that nowadays we ask a great deal of our horses in terms of physical and mental stress, perhaps far more than they were ever intended to cope with. The horse has been specifically bred to retain certain qualities, whilst others have been bred out – this could also be said to be unnatural. So a helping hand from us in the way of a better diet, plus supplements and so on is well deserved.

There are nine golden rules of feeding, upheld and maintained by horsemen through the generations, and more recently upheld by science. They truly are the safe ground rules for feeding. The owner must keep them in mind and in the feed stores.

1 Feed little and often. This is following the horse's own natural pattern. The stomach capacity is proportionately small and its 'J' shape means that it can never be more than two-thirds full. It can cope with a maximum of 5lb (2.27kg) of dry feed at one time. So the amount of food that can be most usefully consumed in one meal is approximately half a bucketful. If fed too much, partially digested food will be pushed out of the stomach which could cause colic.

2 Feed at the same hours every day. The horse is a creature of habit and likes a regular routine. He may fret if his feed is not available when he expects it.

3 Make no sudden changes in the diet. The various bacteria in the horse's gut each feed on a different substance; if the diet is to be changed the bacteria must be given the chance to alter accordingly otherwise the horse will not benefit fully from the feed.

4 Feed plenty of bulk. Fibre in the form of hay and grass are needed in

(page 85) *Steep and rocky ascents and descents are among the variations of terrain likely to be encountered on some of the tough competitive rides (Bob Langrish)*

sufficient quantities – no less than 25 per cent of the daily ration – for a proper digestive process.

5 Feed something succulent every day. This is a good way of boosting appetite and a good source of vitamins and minerals – grass, sliced carrots, apples and so on.

6 Feed only clean, good quality forage. Dust allergies are particularly common among performance horses but can be minimised by using only good quality feedstuffs.

7 Feed according to the individual. You must take into account the work being done, the horse's age, height and temperament.

8 Do not work immediately after feeding. A full stomach puts pressure on the lungs via the diaphragm so the horse cannot fill them properly. When work starts digestion stops, because blood is diverted to the lungs. The average period of retention in the stomach is $1-1\frac{1}{2}$ hours.

9 Water before feeding. If a horse drinks after he has just eaten, some of the food is likely to be washed out of the stomach before it has been properly digested and this may cause colic.

The basic health requirements for a long distance horse are of course the same as for any other horse, and the foundations must be good. What is fed to the horse has a direct bearing on his health and performance – it must provide repair and building material; nourish physical development; and supply energy for work.

To fulfil these needs the horse's diet must contain a number of different nutrients which are categorised under six broad headings: water; protein; carbohydrate; fibre; fats/oils; minerals and vitamins. Each of these six is expressed as a percentage so their total in the nutritional equation must be 100.

· WATER ·

Water or moisture plays several vital roles in the horse's nutrition. It acts as a solvent for carrying nutrients into the horse's system; as saliva it assists in swallowing; it helps give shape to the body cells; it acts as a medium in which digestive chemical reactions can take place; assists in the maintenance of a uniform body temperature and in the removal of surplus heat as sweat; it is the basic ingredient of urine for excreting waste, and of milk for lactating mares.

It is the largest constituent of the body. Between 50 and 80 per cent of the horse's body is made up of water, depending on the animal's age and condition. The younger it is, the more water the body will contain. A loss of only eight per cent of the body's water can cause illness and a loss of 15 per cent can cause dehydration and heat stroke in competition.

Electrolytes can be given neat with a syringe providing that the horse has had plenty to drink (Bob Langrish)

Clean, fresh water should always be available to the horse; in general it drinks between six and ten gallons of water per day. If this is not possible, water at least three times a day in winter and six times a day in summer. Standing water absorbs ammonia and other impurities in the stable so it is best to change it at least twice a day. If the source for this water is the yard trough a separate dipper bucket should be used to fill stable buckets. This will avoid contaminating the water with dirt carried on the bottom of stable buckets.

For horses at grass a stream is ideal, but beware of shallow water on sand because sand in the stomach could cause colic. Troughs are good providing they are filled from a pipe and have an outlet to allow them to be regularly emptied and cleaned, and will not become filled with dead leaves etc.

The exact quantity of water the horse drinks depends on the individual and the type of food he has – a horse on dry feed will drink more – also on the work he is doing, and the weather.

During a competition offer water if you can every two hours, or allow the horse to drink from puddles or streams. It is important for a long distance horse to be constantly 'topped' up to prevent dehydration. If he does become dehydrated after a ride, he should be offered a limited quantity of water every ten minutes until he has satisfied his thirst. It should not be given to him all in one go. Never allow him to drink too much at once, particularly if you intend to go on and do any fast work. Water is heavy and a full stomach will put pressure on the diaphragm and make breathing difficult.

It is a good idea to take your own water to a competition in containers, and re-fill them from a tap rather than a 'public' trough where germs could be picked up. It is common practice to use electrolytes which are added to the drinking water. These contain essential minerals, particularly salt, to make up for those lost in sweat. They can prevent dehydration by helping the gut transport water to the blood and body tissues and are available with or without glucose which also aids water uptake. Some horses object to sweet-tasting water, but could also be offered a bucket of plain water so they can choose according to their needs.

· PROTEIN ·

Proteins are the body's building blocks, important for the development of bone, muscles, blood cells, hormones and most constituents of the body, and for the repair and replacement of worn muscle tissues lost through natural wastage. They can also help the horse to develop optimum resistance to disease.

Protein requirements are increased in the long distance horse due to the sustained exercise and stress. But although it is a source of energy, protein will only be used in the absence of carbohydrates or fats. Horses can tolerate higher protein levels providing that the carbohydrate/fat balance is maintained and vitamins fed accordingly. But protein is expensive and the horse has to use energy to break down and remove any excess, so it is uneconomical to feed too much.

The body-building constituents of proteins are amino acids, and it is these that are absorbed across the small intestine wall. There are about 23 different amino acids, of which ten are 'essential'; these include lysine, methionine and tryptophan.

To discover the protein content of food, analyse it for nitrogen, since in general, protein contains 16 per cent nitrogen. This percentage expresses the amount of crude protein. Not all of this substance can be digested by the horse, so feed tables specify the amount which is digestible, and this is shown as digestible crude protein – DCP.

· CARBOHYDRATES ·

Carbohydrates form the basis of the horse's source of energy. They include substances such as starch and sugar, and make up a large proportion of the horse's diet.

Starch is from plants, particularly roots and tubers. Cereal grains contain just over 10 per cent starch and are a good and readily available source of starch for the horse.

Sugar is the simplest form of carbohydrate, and breaks down into monosaccharides, or glucose, and is absorbed through the wall of the small intestine. Glucose is stored in the body as glycogen and fat which can later be converted back into glucose to be used as energy in the muscles. If the horse is fed too much carbohydrate, problems such as laminitis, lymphangitis and azoturia can be caused.

· FIBRE ·

Fibre, or cellulose, is classed as carbohydrate or roughage, and plays an essential role in the horse's metabolism. It helps break down and digest other feeds, and helps maintain the balance of bacteria in the gut. The term fibre actually refers to the structure found in plant cell walls. It is broken down in the caecum and large intestine and can be an important source of energy for the grass-kept horse. The diet must consist of no less than 17 per cent of fibre.

Grazing is an inherent need for the horse, which is, after all, a mobile herbivore. This digestive system, in particular the hind gut, is suited to the horse's natural state in the wild. It eats the tips of grass and can immediately utilise the simple sugars they contain to provide energy for a fast turn of speed which is its only defence in the face of danger. The upper part of the stomach has evolved to convert starches, sugars and amino acids quickly into readily available nutrients.

Because of the horse's need to graze, the upper gut is small. But if the animal comes across any indigestible matter, this is passed through to the enlarged caecum and colon to undergo a more rigorous degradation in the fermentation process involving bacteria.

The bacteria in the gut is another very important factor to consider when feeding the horse. Some nutritionalists actually talk about feeding the bacteria as opposed to feeding the horse! The bacteria break down the cellulose and hemi-cellulose, the fibrous part of the plant. So, to help these bacteria thrive and to keep a good balance the horse must have good fibre – hay for example. Without it the horse could not survive. Even decreasing the amount of fibre in the horse's diet can lead to problems.

· FATS/OILS ·

Fats are a good source of heat and energy for the horse. They are easily stored throughout the body and in particular in the liver, and also provide insulation as subcutaneous fat. They make a very useful addition to the diet of the endurance horse and some feed manufacturers are now adding fat to their high performance horse feeds.

Some fats have a greater digestibility than others – the oil in alfalfa or lucerne is only 39 per cent, while the oil in corn oil is as much as 90 per cent. Other oils, castor oil for instance, are indigestible.

Research at the University of Kentucky in America has shown that diets supplemented with corn oil have proved very palatable and highly digestible to the horse. Because of its high energy make-up horses on this diet were found to eat less feed, but were able to maintain constant bodyweight with no adverse effect on their performance.

The digestion of fat is helped by lecithin, nature's fat emulsifier, which is contained in a variety of cereals and most feeds.

· MINERALS ·

Minerals play various roles in the horse's bodily functions; it is important to have the correct balance of minerals which must include calcium and phosphorus.

· CALCIUM AND PHOSPHORUS ·

Calcium is important for bone formation, blood clotting and for nerve function, and is found in grass, bone meal, ground chalk or limestone.

Phosphorus is also needed for bone formation and is a vital component of many of the essential chemicals in the body. It can be found in grass and grain.

The two go hand in hand but calcium should be in the highest proportion, 2–1; an imbalance, or too little calcium, and the effectiveness is limited. Hay has more calcium than phosphorus, and cereals vice versa. Bran inhibits the uptake of calcium so a supplement would be advisable for a horse with bran in its diet. The effectiveness of both minerals is dependent on vitamin D, obtained from sunlight.

Calcium is being constantly replaced in the bones. Research has shown that the deposition in bone is decreased by as much as 20 per cent in a long distance horse. This triggers reduced calcium excretion in the urine and increased body retention.

· SODIUM & POTASSIUM ·

Sodium and potassium are also important to the horse as they help control the fluid balance in the body, and help in blood formation and digestion of food.

A normal diet is high in potassium and low in sodium. Both are lost during prolonged sweating, so give extra salt either in the form of electrolytes or table salt, the latter at a rate of 1–2oz (30–60g) per day in the feed. A deficiency can manifest itself as tiredness.

· *IODINE* ·

Iodine is part of the hormone thyroxine which governs the rate of metabolism. A deficiency causes listlessness.

· *SELENIUM* ·

A supplement containing selenium with vitamin E can be given to endurance horses; this is thought to help prevent cell damage, particularly in the muscle. Selenium also helps horses which are prone to azoturia.

· *IRON* ·

Iron, together with copper, is essential for the formation of blood pigment (haemoglobin) which carries oxygen in the blood. A good, balanced diet will normally contain all the iron that the horse requires; as are also magnesium, needed for teeth and bone development; and manganese and zinc, used for breaking up food in digestion.

VITAMINS

· *VITAMIN A* ·

This is utilised by the horse for vision and bone and tissue growth. It is obtained from carotene which is absorbed and stored in the liver. This is found in grass and green foods so a horse which does not have access to grazing may need a vitamin A supplement, cod liver oil for example.

· *VITAMIN B* ·

This vitamin is complex and includes vitamin B1 which plays an important role in energy production in the cells. Without it lactic and pyruvic acid cannot be broken down, resulting in a build-up of these acids and a drop in blood glucose levels. B1 is found in cereals.

As a group, the B vitamins can be found in fresh herbage and protein rich foods, and are synthesised in the gut. They help in the utilisation of carbohydrates and nutrients.

· *VITAMIN C* ·

This is ascorbic acid, which is involved in certain immune responses to viruses. The horse produces its own supplies but these may be reduced if the horse is under stress, and then the horse is at risk of disease.

· *VITAMIN D* ·

This vitamin is obtained from sunlight and is used by the gut to help absorb calcium and phosphorus. A deficiency can lead to problems in the bones. It is stored in the liver; a supplement can be provided in the form of cod liver oil in the winter when the stores may be used up.

· *VITAMIN E* ·

This vitamin works in conjunction with selenium and can be a treatment for azoturia. It also helps the body utilise fats, so if extra fats are given in the diet it is recommended that an increased amount of vitamin E is fed.

ENERGY

The most important factor to be considered in nutrition is energy. As the work load of the horse increases so he will need more energy giving foods. However, it is hard to assess the exact amount of energy that the horse is actually obtaining from his food, and so it may be difficult to feed the correct amount.

A resting, stabled adult horse of 880lb (400kg) (eg 14hh–15hh Arab or 14hh–14.2hh Thoroughbred type) requires 50 mega-joules (MJ) of digestible energy every day, a 1,100lb (500kg) horse needs 69MJ, and a 1,320lb (600kg) horse needs 79MJ. The amount of MJ needed does not increase in direct relation to weight – a horse that is fifty per cent heavier does not necessarily need fifty per cent more energy. Energy is found in proteins, fats, fibre, carbohydrates, and is measured in mega-calories or mega-joules of digestible energy, ie MCDE or MJDE.

Because the endurance horse has an increased level of physical activity sustained over longer periods of time, he needs a greater amount of stored energy than a horse in light work. But it is difficult to provide him with enough since the maximum dry matter consumption is approximately 2.5–3.0 per cent of body weight. For instance, an 880lb (400kg) endurance horse can eat only about 26lb (12kg) of dry feed per day. A solution could be to feed fats, which weight for weight provide two-and-a-half times the amount of energy provided by carbohydrates.

Carbohydrate loading, typical of the diet of human marathon runners, is unsuitable for horses for at least two reasons: it predisposes to azoturia; and in comparison humans work on a much higher glucose level than horses – glucose is the sole energy source for the brain and central nervous system, but most other systems in the horse utilise fat. In addition, the level of glucose in the muscle in horses is naturally much higher than in humans so there is little point in over-loading the system with starch. It is, in fact, difficult to feed a good carbohydrate source and the whole subject is quite controversial.

Protein is also a good source of energy, providing about 10 to 15 per cent, but unlike fats cannot be stored by the horse.

It is particularly important for an endurance horse that he has reserves of energy in store to call upon in his sustained effort, and many feeding experts suggest that the only way to get the horse to store a large enough amount of energy is to store fats.

· USING FATS ·

Having fed extra fat (eg corn or soya bean oil) it is important that the horse can convert it. The primary storage centre for fat is in the liver; it is also stored around the body, particularly in the muscle cells – each cell has mitochondria, which are the cell's incinerators for 'burning' energy.

The fats (lipids) must be taken to the mitochondria from the storage sources, and this is done via metabolic 'pathways' which are opened up through training the horse. An unfit horse would use protein from the muscle, as this would provide the energy required although it would result in muscular stiffness.

The horse does not have a gall bladder but it is very tolerant of fat, and can apparently cope with being fed more; vitamin E is needed to help the body absorb it, so make sure that this is present in the diet if greater amounts are fed. However, it is pointless putting potential energy in if the horse is not going to make use of it. So, you ought only to feed fat when the horse is in training and the metabolic pathways are open, and some would argue that there is no point in feeding it except in the build-up to a competition.

Nutritional science has recently discovered a simple substance called L-carnitine which makes a significant difference in the transportation of fats. Though also known as vitamin BT, it is a vitamin-like substance rather than a true vitamin and is synthesised in the body. Much research is currently being done into it particularly in relation to the energy needs of high performance horses.

It transfers fat across the wall of the mitochondria into the cell's incinerators. In the process of fat 'burning' (or fat metabolism), L-carnitine is changed from 'free carnitine' into what is known as 'acetyl-carnitine' – the L-carnitine is soaked up in the fat.

It is therefore very important in the body and, since it is constantly being produced, it is essential that the horse's diet contains good protein, iron, vitamin B6 and vitamin C.

It is known that an L-carnitine deficiency can stop the stroke of the heart and make the animal very lethargic. Incidentally those early sailors who were thought to have died of scurvy due simply to vitamin C deficiency, in fact died of acetyl-carnitine deficiency, the result of not having enough vitamin C for its manufacture.

One of the most useful things about L-carnitine is that it can get over the problem of sub-maximum training, that is, in an under-trained horse it can clear the pathways which would otherwise have to be achieved by good training.

Whether or not L-carnitine needs to be fed to the horse still remains to be seen. Work done with marathon runners and older athletes (men of about 50) doing the London marathon, showed that giving them 'free carnitine loading' resulted in a quick recovery rate.

STRESS

When working out the energy requirements of the horse the stress factor must be taken into consideration. Stress can cause enormous problems since in training, almost every part of the body system is under some form of stress, and even minor changes in the diet can disrupt the digestion process.

The heart is the most important organ and in the endurance horse it can be under the greatest stress. It is interesting to note that the energy utilised by the heart is almost exclusively confined to fats, so acetyl-carnitine will help strengthen the heart. But do remember that you can over-load the heart with fats so it is very important to get the rations right. Nutrition is about balance and you cannot take one thing out of context.

Pro-biotics is about the nurturing of live bacteria in the gut, and this is very important because it keeps the correct balance in the horse's body. A diet which is high in fibre, nitrogen (a form of protein), plus a certain amount of starch, will help counteract stress because the bacteria which help to keep the horse's system in balance will be fed correctly. Ideally, feed a mixture of raw and cooked foods.

With the long distance horse it is important to feed the most degradable foods which will take up the least amount of space. Nutritionists work on a figure of M/D, the dry matter of the food divided into the amount of energy it provides – the drier the M/D the more concentrated the diet is.

Super bacteria of 'super bugs' have been produced which can be introduced into the horse's gut to then take over the other bacteria or work alongside them, to perform a better function. To explain, when a foal is born he is completely sterile, but from the moment he suckles from his mother he starts to accumulate bacteria, good and bad, from teats, hay and other aspects of his new environment.

The super bacteria, mixed with water in a powder form, may be fed to the potential performance horse soon after birth mixed with water. The bacteria will multiply and thrive in the horse's body. Super bacteria may also be given to the adult horse in times of stress. Much research is still being done into this aspect of feeding horses with a view to better performance.

WEIGHT

Regularly weighing your horse will help you find his optimum performance weight, and is well worth doing if you are really serious about the fitness of your horse in relation to the way you are feeding him and his health. A slight drop in weight could highlight a viral infection before it starts. You can weigh him, for a fee, at your local public weighbridge, or perhaps a local haulage firm might have one on the premises. You could also use a weigh tape, although this is less accurate.

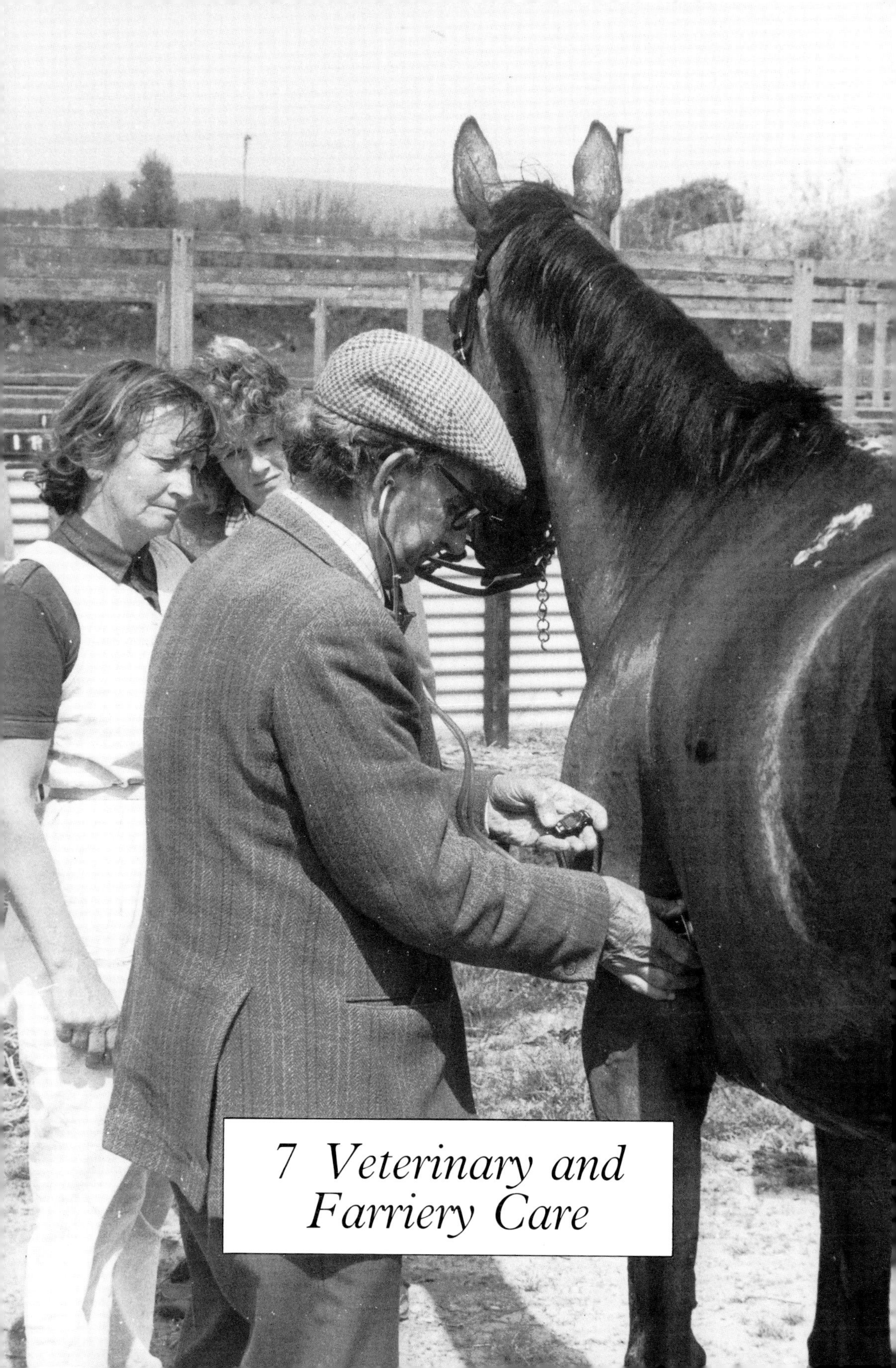
7 Veterinary and
Farriery Care

All hands on deck to cool Tarim. Val Long's crew hard at work with water and sponges at the end of a hot and tough Golden Horseshoe ride (Bob Langrish)

VETERINARY JUDGING

Veterinary inspections are an integral part of long distance rides: the horse must be fit enough at the start to do the distance it has been entered for, and not in any distress at the finish because of what it has done. Inspections are made before the start of the ride, towards the end of any compulsory halts, and thirty minutes after the finish. The purpose of these inspections is for the vet to oversee the welfare of the horse. If he sees a horse which he feels is unfit he can advise its withdrawal. On tougher rides where peak performance must be achieved the horse will need to be stressed to some extent, and the greater the stress the greater the veterinary control required.

· PRE-RIDE ·

This initial inspection is to make sure that the animal is fit enough to start and capable of carrying his rider. Its purpose is also to establish the base line parameters (ie heart rate) from which changes in the horse's condition can be measured. The pulse should lie between 36 and 42 beats per minute and the respiratory rate is usually between 8 and 14 cycles per minute.

The heart rate is taken using a watch with a second hand and a stethoscope. The base pulse rate is used in CTRs as the criterion for awarding gradings, as the recovery rate is judged by its closeness to the base rate. The normal heart rate may be higher or lower than the average rate – 36 is low and 42 is high.

The horse must be trotted up so that his action can be checked for any peculiarities which will be noted down for the vet to refer to at the end of the ride. Any significant changes would then be classed as lameness. Usually you will be asked to run the horse up and back along a road, or trot a figure of eight. Have your horse trotting freely on a loose rein beside you; as you reach the turn, slow down to walk and push the horse round away from you, and trot on again once you are facing in the right direction. Practise this at home.

If your horse has a peculiar action two vets may want to watch him. Lameness is the most common reason for elimination during post-ride vet inspections.

A thorough examination is made for current injuries. The vet will look at the horse's mouth for lesions, and the back and girth areas for sores and galls. These checks ensure that they are not confused as damage sustained on the ride. Fresh or raw galls may result in the rider being penalised or eliminated.

The vet must make a general mental note about the horse so that he can spot any difference at the end of the ride. A vet writer accompanying the vet will note down the appropriate details.

· HALF-WAY HALT ·

A vet may be on hand at the entrance of the half-way halt to assess the apparent condition of your horse as you ride in.

You and your helper must then attend to the horse. The procedure for horse care is similar to that at the end of the ride. Loosen the girth but do not remove the saddle straightaway. Allow the horse to drink and pick at grass. Sponge water over his neck, lower chest and legs.

Vetting takes place 20 minutes after your arrival at the halt. A full examination is made and the pulse and respiratory rates are measured. To continue a BHS or EHPS ride the pulse rate must be 64 or lower. The horse is then trotted up and checked over for leg wounds, and for any lesions, old and new.

· FINAL VETTING ·

A vet may be at the finish line to make a general assessment as to whether help is needed. The thirty minutes before the final vetting must be used to cool the horse and get him comfortable, treating any cuts if necessary. There is then a thorough examination of the horse in

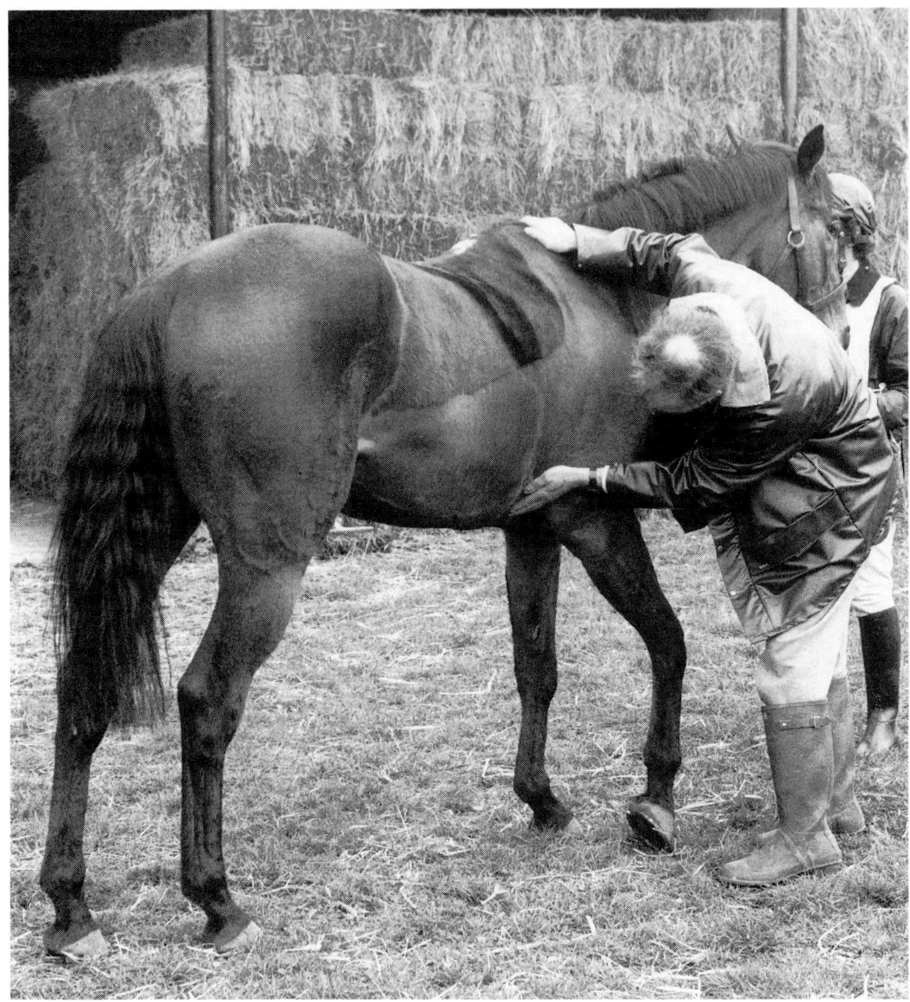

Feeling for signs of girth galls behind the elbow

the same sequence as on the pre-ride check. The pulse is checked first: on EHPS rides, a high pulse rate is penalised according to the number of counts it is above the individual horse's base rate. If the heart rate is more than 64 the horse is eliminated. If the respiratory rate is giving cause for concern, for instance if the respiration is more than the heart rate, the horse will be eliminated.

On a CTR, penalties can also be given for saddle sores, girth galls, mouth lesions and lost shoes, on a scale of one to ten for each injury. Minor scratches or cuts may not be penalised if the vet considers that they are not self-inflicted nor causing discomfort. Lameness results in automatic elimination.

In FEI competitions the final vetting is five hours after the ride is completed.

· *VET GATES* ·

At vet gates on endurance rides the onus is on the rider to present the horse to the vet when the parameters for the ride have been attained. Once this is verified, and the horse has been confirmed sound, horse and rider can continue on the ride.

On your arrival, the vet will take a brief look for exhaustion, lameness or more serious injuries. The horse may be presented for vetting at any time up to 20 minutes after arrival; if it passes the set parameters it will immediately undergo a one minute test. The heart rate is taken and must be under 64; the horse is then trotted up over a measured distance of 30 metres and back. A stop-watch records one minute from the time he starts to trot, and the heart rate is taken again after exactly one minute and must be 64 or below.

If the horse fails he may be re-presented provided it is within ten minutes of arrival. But if he is presented ten minutes *after* arrival and fails, he will be eliminated. There is a minimum of two vet gates on a ride.

Incidentally, many wrongly assume that trotting up increases the horse's heart rate, but in fact it has been proved that it has the opposite effect.

CARE OF THE HORSE AFTER RIDE
· *PRE-VET*

Once you are over the finish line your task is to make your horse comfortable, cool him off and encourage him to relax so that his pulse rate returns to normal. This is when you really must spring into action with renewed energy, however tired or emotional you are yourself. On longer rides you will have a crew so you can leave much of the work to them. Relax if possible, and compose yourself ready for the veterinary judging half-an-hour after you finish.

How you go about preparing the horse for the vet will depend on the weather and the state of your horse. In hot weather the horse will need to be washed over with plenty of cool water.

Do not remove the saddle straightaway – loosen the girth and release the pressure on the back and girth area gradually. This will reduce the risk of oedema and pressure bumps which are difficult to get rid of in the short time you have before the final vetting. Take off the bridle and replace with a halter, sponging away sweat marks.

Pick out the feet so that you remove any stones, and have the foot clean for the vet to look at.

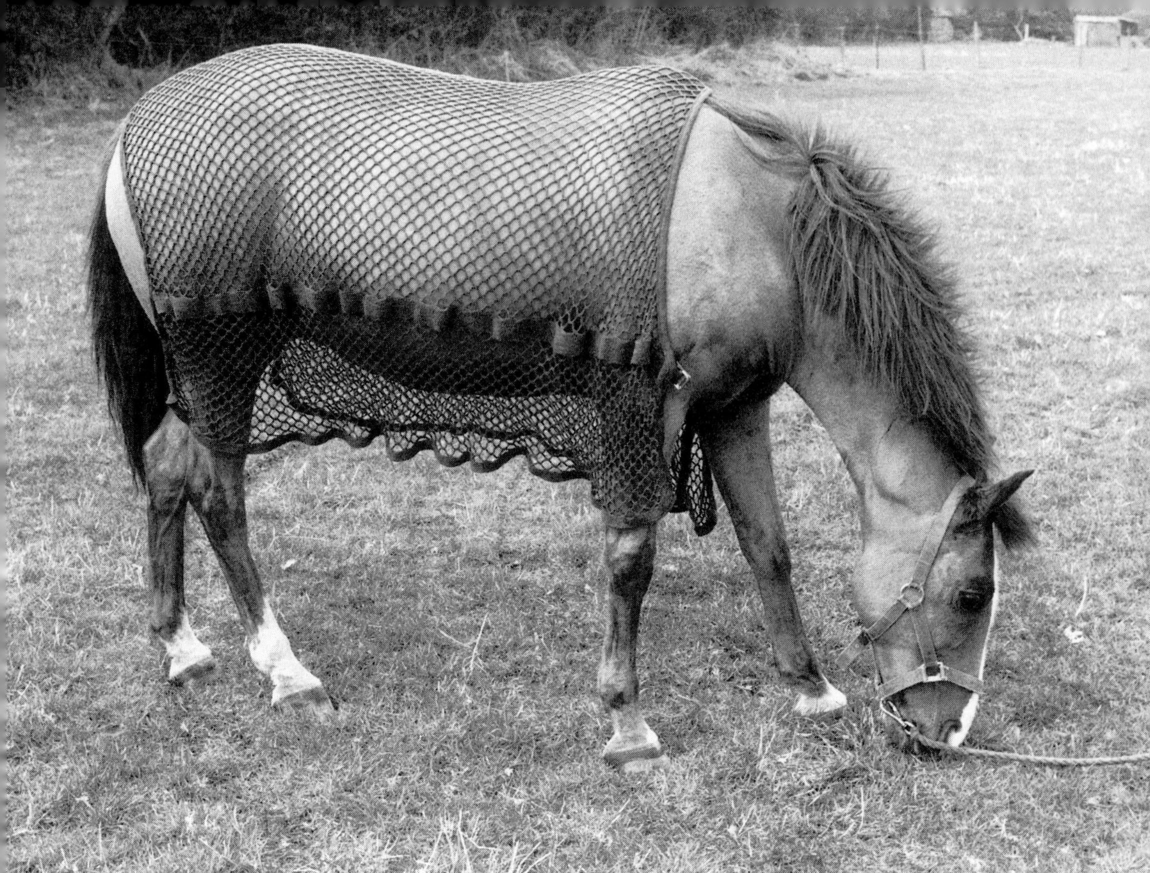

This horse is being allowed to 'wind down' naturally by grazing (Steve Moore)

Allow the horse to drink freely. If it is a cool day rug up the back and loins. Walk the horse for a few minutes to keep the muscles warm and prevent them stiffening up, then allow him to graze quietly, so that he relaxes. Grazing restores the electrolyte and water balance naturally.

· POST-VET ·

Once home give the horse a good deep bed and water; do not feed for at least two to three hours after a ride – by then the blood supply will have returned to the gut and there should be less risk of colic. It is often best to give a light mash.

The horse should be groomed and rugged with the minimum fuss; bandages will help to prevent the legs from filling. An astringent paste can be used to reduce minor swellings, but not if there are any open wounds. Keep an eye on him but don't keep fussing – allow him to relax and 'wind down'. Last thing at night check that there is no sign of colic.

The following morning check your horse over thoroughly. Keep an eye out for puffiness in the legs – the tendons should stand out clearly. Any swelling around the fetlock joint must not be ignored – the cause might be the hard ground the day before, a strain or a knock. Walk the horse out, even trot him up, to check that all is well. Treat strains and bruises as necessary.

If you have been taking part in a major ride, particularly a race ride, spend the night afterwards at the venue. This allows plenty of time for the horse to recover; travelling is also a form of work for him, so bandage the legs for the journey as tired legs are more likely to suffer damage.

FATIGUE AND ASSOCIATED CONDITIONS

Fatigue is the inability to continue to work at a desired speed and accuracy, and is nature's way of telling the body to slow down. This does not mean that the horse must necessarily be stopped. He can continue so long as the rider takes care that his condition does not deteriorate to a severe state of exhaustion where medical treatment is needed. Fatigue is caused by:

1 The using up of muscle glycogen stores during prolonged steady work.
2 Dehydration due to excessive sweating, leading to a drop in blood volume and therefore poor blood flow to muscles and other organs.
3 The accumulation of lactic acid within muscle fibres during fast work (azoturia).
4 Lameness, altering the normal gait and placing abnormal strains on muscles and bones.

So, watch out for any signs of fatigue and be willing to respond. The warning signs begin with mental attitude: he may lose his zest, and be indifferent about being overtaken by other horses; he may be having to put more than his usual effort into ascending hills. As he becomes more tired a series of subtle changes will occur in his gait.

Each gait has an individual metabolic requirement from the body – it needs a differing amount of energy to propel the horse along at the same velocity. If given the chance to choose for himself, the horse will slow down to a gait which is more economical in its demands on the body. He may change his leading leg which will help reduce fatigue.

The rider might do several things to encourage the horse forward and thereby assess his level of fatigue. He may pick up but his quickening of pace will last for an increasingly shorter period of time as he tires. If the rider needs to nag at him and perhaps resort to the whip, then the horse is showing that he really is tired and would like to stick to the pace he chooses.

If he continues to ask his muscles for more effort, then problems arise. His co-ordination will deteriorate resulting in extra strain on his system. If the rider still pushes him on the horse will be in some danger. The respiration may reach a higher level than the pulse – he then becomes completely unresponsive, his eyes will become dull and glazed, and his movements poor and unco-ordinated. By this time he will effectively be out of the competition.

In a horse suffering from fatigue the pulse and respiration rates will remain high for at least 30 minutes. (In fact, it may actually increase during rest over this period.) A horse, which after 30 minutes still has a pulse rate markedly above 60 beats per minute, is showing very definite signs of fatigue.

AZOTURIA
(exertional rhabdomyolysis, set-fast or tying up)

The immediate signs of azoturia are that the horse will sweat excessively and be unable to walk forward, or will do so with difficulty. He may blow or hyperventilate, and will adopt an uncomfortable gait, moving stiffly behind – it may feel as though the horse wants to stop to urinate.

The muscles of the loin and hindquarters will feel hard and painful to touch. If forced to go on the horse may be distressed by the pain, and the hind legs may even become paralysed. Dark red or brownish urine may be passed, although in severe cases no urine is passed at all. If very badly affected the horse will collapse completely.

Glycogen in the muscles is converted during exercise into lactic acid. In cases of azoturia, the lactic acid is not removed quickly enough and accumulates in the muscles, causing them to seize up. It is sometimes compared to an attack of cramp but in fact is far more serious because the fall in pH results in the destruction of the muscle fibres to some degree.

In long distance riding azoturia almost invariably occurs because the muscles are not adequately prepared for the work required of them, both in the short term (warming up) and the long term (muscle development). It is advisable to walk or trot for the first few miles of a competition ride, unless the horse has been warmed up for 15–20 minutes before starting. If you leave the start and go fast up a hill then you are asking for trouble. Vets adjudicating on Exmoor, for instance, have been able to go out and literally calculate the point where horses are likely to develop azoturia.

It is a mistake to think that, with 50 miles still to go, you are conserving the horse's energy by doing nothing until you start – and then going 'hell for leather' off up a hill. The horse doesn't know whether he has got 50 miles to go or four. What has happened is that he has had to adapt from doing absolutely nothing to being worked very hard for a long period of time, and at a certain point is unable to cope. That is how problems occur.

Cases of azoturia inevitably happen in the first three miles or so of a ride. They can also happen towards the end of a long ride as a result of fatigue. It is a syndrome with a complex number of causes and is nothing like as well defined as people often imagine.

The treatment of azoturia is controversial because it must take into consideration all the factors contributing to the particular case. There are a wide variety of reasons for doing one thing and not doing another. Basically, treatment is aimed at helping the body systems to function as normally as possible until recovery has been achieved; this is done by expelling as many of the waste products as fast as possible. Plenty of fluids should be given, if necessary intravenously or via a stomach tube.

If your horse feels as though he is tying up you *must* stop and keep the horse still, keep the muscles warmed, and get some help. If the weather is warm, head for a shady spot, providing you don't have far to go, and ideally somewhere with water.

In mild cases you can often walk the horse round to ease the symptoms, but before doing so it is better to wait for professional advice. Only once the horse appears to have recovered should you attempt to go on. If the horse has developed clinical signs of azoturia it must not be allowed to continue under any circumstances. It will require at least several days to recover, depending on severity.

If you continue it will make things far worse – after all, it is a potentially fatal condition. Do not struggle on to the next checkpoint. Send word with another rider and the vet should come to you.

Transport should also be sent out to take the horse back and it should not be exercised or taken home until the veterinary surgeon says that it is safe to do so. Travelling will stress the horse further.

The horse should be rested for a few days, depending on how much damage there is. The vet can judge the extent of the damage by measuring the muscle enzyme levels.

If you detect the initial signs of muscle stiffness the answer is to slow right down and keep the horse walking. At this stage it is best to keep the muscles working; they should recover with a short period of 'ticking over' and become attuned to the work, and then away you can go again. Those riders who are sufficiently sensitive will not allow the horse to get into that situation in the first place.

· DEHYDRATION ·

Dehydration occurs to some extent on all rides under all conditions. It is likely to become a clinically significant problem if the horse has been sweating heavily but has not been able to get enough to drink. Fluid can be lost in both sweating and respiration (transpiration).

Even in cool weather a horse will sweat six to eight litres an hour at a steady canter. He can cope with this providing there is low humidity and he is given plenty of opportunity to drink.

Sweating is the body's heat regulation system and the fluid emitted from the skin contains natural electrolytes (body salts) including sodium chloride, potassium and calcium. A potassium deficiency will lead to muscle weakness and exhaustion. Once the fluid levels have become depleted the horse finds it difficult to remove body heat and as a result may suffer from heat stroke.

In the early stages of dehydration the horse becomes dull and lethargic, with a high pulse rate of 60 or 70 plus which, together with the respiration rate, takes a long time to return to normal. In severe cases the skin dries out and the eyes sink back into their sockets. The mucus membranes change from being light pink to red, and the horse has a high temperature.

At this stage the horse is likely to become disorientated. He may have muscle tremors in the flanks, and develop colic. He will be unable to sweat and the skin dries quickly. The horse will be immobile and may even be down.

A useful, though not scientifically accurate, method of judging dehydration, is to take up a pinch of skin on the neck: when you let go, the longer it takes for the skin to go back down and return to normal, the more dehydrated the horse is. However, for some horses it is quite normal for the skin to take a long time to revert.

Another method of assessing dehydration is to measure the capillary refill time. Press the horse's gum hard with one finger. When you take your finger off you will find that there is a white mark which returns to pink when the pressure is removed. The slower this is to recover, the more dehydrated the horse is. When the time exceeds two seconds there is cause for concern.

In mild cases, the horse can be allowed to drink up to one gallon of water every 15 minutes. If he is used to it, give him water with electrolytes mixed in, otherwise he must be encouraged to drink plain water.

When given in water, the electrolyte solution should not be over-concentrated otherwise there is an osmotic affect. What happens is that fluid is sucked out of the bloodstream – where it is needed to maintain the blood volume – and transferred to the gut; this further dehydrates the horse. Electrolytes can be given neat with a syringe but this should only be done if the horse has sufficient water in the gut to absorb them, for the same reason.

Many horses will only drink regularly after the first 20 or 30 miles. It should be part of the horse's training, to get him to drink when water is offered and to persuade him to drink water

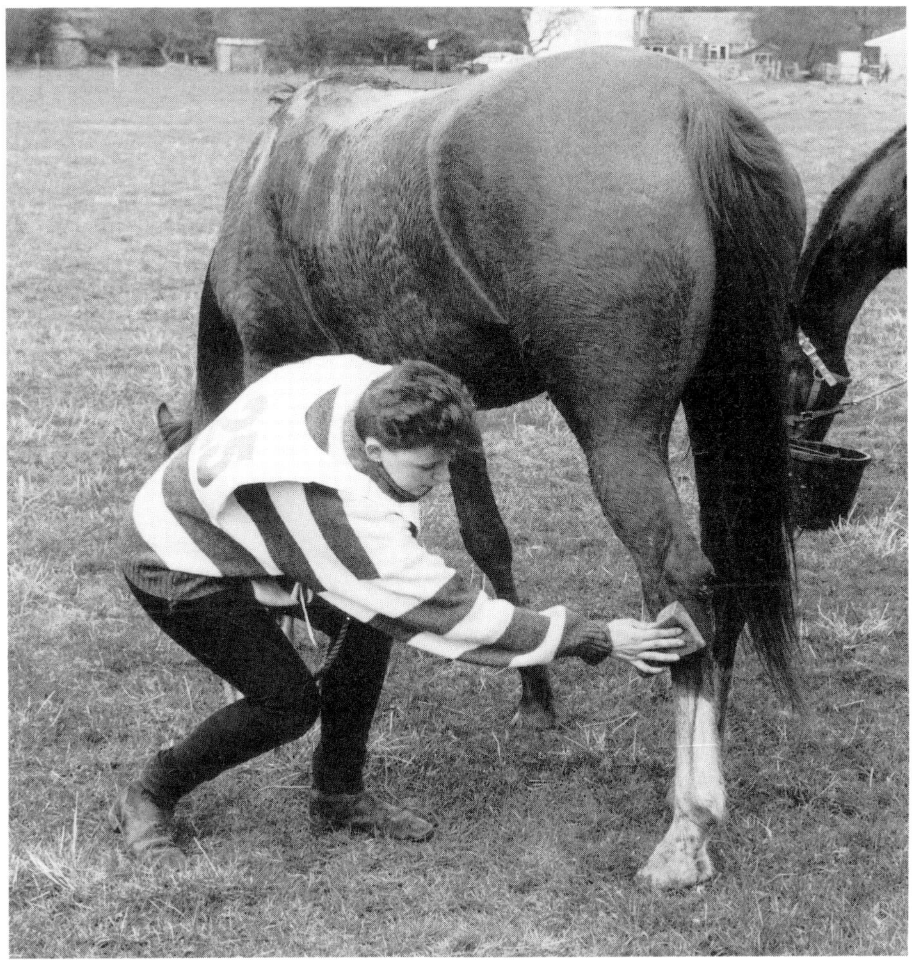

Sponging down after a ride also allows the rider to check for any cuts or wounds
(Steve Moore)

with electrolytes mixed in; that way you can maintain the body salts as well as the fluid.

Encourage your horse to drink at streams but don't expect him to drink straightaway. Allow him a bit of time. Sometimes horses will drink, then pause and look around before drinking again. The desire to drink is often disturbed by other horses moving away, so when you are moving away from others in a stream leave as slowly and quietly as you can. Better still, wait for the group to finish.

If your horse won't drink, then the next best thing is to tip the water over him because then at least you are keeping him cool. On a hot or humid day horses should be regularly sponged with water to prevent them overheating. If you throw cold water

107

over the large muscle masses then you must keep the horse moving afterwards.

· *COLIC* ·

Colic, or abdominal pain, occurs when the waves of contraction and relaxation rhythmically passing along the bowel (peristalsis) are interrupted. This causes some areas of the bowel to be distended or stretched, causing pain.

Unfortunately, the horse's system can be disturbed by a change in routine; travelling for example. If your horse suffers colic before a competition you may be faced with something of a dilemma: the vet may want to give him a drug to treat it, but you will be disqualified if that particular drug is not permitted under the competition rules.

Exhaustion and dehydration can lead to colic. One of the main causes is a reduced blood supply to the gut, because so much has been diverted to other parts of the body, particularly the muscles. A problem with dehydration is that although fluid can be added to the gut there is no blood supply there to absorb it. Once the blood volume is back to normal some of it will go back to the gut and the colic will be eased.

Once the horse has stopped working there will be a gradual return to normal, although you must establish the volume of the blood before you can go any further. This is one of the reasons why it is so important to keep the horse drinking throughout a ride.

There are a few other specific conditions which may be encountered with horses suffering from exhaustion, – 'thumps' is one, synchronous diaphragmatic flutter similar to hiccups. However, they cannot be isolated from exhaustion and are part of the same complex.

LAMENESS

Lameness can range from ruptured tendons, fractured bone or to a stone in the foot. Foot lameness is most common.

If the horse is in pain but there is no obvious cause, the lameness will probably increase if the horse continues the ride. Dismount and have a look. If you can, continue by leading the horse slowly for a short distance. Should the lameness continue, stop and call for help, but if it decreases you should be able to continue carefully.

Lameness can be divided into two categories, poor risk and good risk.

Poor risk lameness includes tendon, ligament and joint lesions, and continuing the ride is likely to cause further serious damage. Tendon injuries usually occur when muscles become tired. Tendons join muscle to bone, and the muscle acts as a shock absorber during movement. When tired the 'spring' effect is reduced, and this results in the tendon fibres tearing due to the extra strain. Usually it only occurs in the flexor tendons of the foreleg.

Muscle tiredness can be minimalised in the following ways:

1 Making sure that the horse is fit enough to complete the ride.
2 Making sure that the rider is fit too. A tired rider will lose balance and become an increasingly difficult burden on the horse, causing muscle strain.
3 Maintaining a steady pace. Going fast then slowing to recover, then going fast again, will only cause problems. Stick to the most suitable pace or mph for the competition and terrain.
4 Warm the horse up properly before the ride and build up the speed gradually on the first few miles. This helps to prime the muscles for the task ahead and opens up the correct metabolic pathways for maximum efficiency.

Ligament injuries are usually incurred over rough ground when the horse is tired. The ligaments join bone to bone, and in most cases support the joint. Abnormal joint movements are controlled in the fit horse by muscles but this does not happen when the horse is tired.

The same circumstances can cause joint injuries. Over difficult, sticky terrain the top end of the leg could be put under pressure and pulled away while the lower leg is left behind. More often the foot is twisted on sticky or rocky ground. Training over rough terrain can help build up strength in the legs and will help to improve the horse's confidence over such ground. Careful riding can save many such injuries.

If you find yourself in a situation where your horse has one of these injuries then you really should not continue. Depending on its severity you can walk your horse to a suitable point or get somebody to come out and pick you up.

Good risk lameness includes cuts, bruises, corns and muscle soreness, and the ride is not likely to cause any further damage.

Bruising of the feet usually causes lameness for a few strides, then the horse will recover. Again, training over similar conditions will help harden up the soles.

Corns often form as a result of poor shoeing and can be avoided by having the horse re-shod a few days before the ride, ensuring that the shoes are not too short at the heels.

Muscle soreness is difficult to assess but should not affect one leg more than another. A degree of soreness is permissible, depending on the severity of the ride.

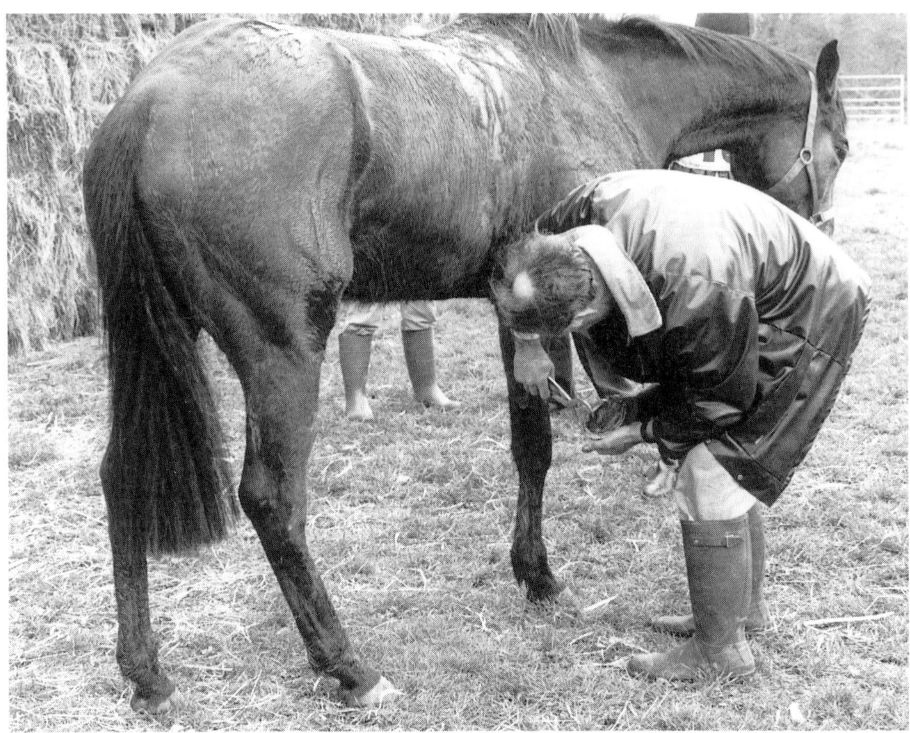

Using veterinary pincers to check for bruising in the feet (Steve Moore)

For any lameness, dismount and take a look. If there is nothing obvious, then walk the horse for a short distance – if it recovers you can continue carefully.

Brushing injuries tend to occur when the horse is tired, and when he has difficult or very heavy going to cope with.

· FOOT INJURIES ·

A vet will check the foot for sore areas by using a set of hoof testers (pincers), with which he squeezes the heel and sole areas.

Puncture wounds in the foot can develop into abscesses. If the sole is punctured the infection builds up under it and cannot escape because the original hole closes up quite quickly. This build-up of pus is very painful, and although the foot is sometimes hot, there is often nothing to see on the outside. The vet or farrier must remove the shoe and pare out the tender area until the site of the puncture wound is revealed; a sharp knife will then be used to release the pus. Poultices will keep it clean, increase the blood supply to the area and draw all the infected material out. The horse may be given an antibiotic, but must be covered against tetanus.

A bruised sole is clinically similar to pus in the foot: the leg does not swell, there is no penetration of the sole, but there will be a reaction to pressure, although a reddened area on the sole may take some days to appear. The foot may take some time to recover.

A corn is a form of bruising at a particular site and it may become infected. The shoe must be removed and the sole at the seat of the corn may be pared lightly, cutting down towards the reddened area. The foot should be poulticed. When the horse is re-shod your farrier may suggest that a three-quarter or a set shoe be used.

· GIRTH-GALLS ·

Girth galls form where the girth has pinched the skin and starved the tissues of blood. Horses with sensitive skin may be particularly prone to them.

Treat any lumps straightaway to prevent them from getting worse. Bathe with a warm, salt water solution, and dry with cotton wool. Apply antiseptic powder; after that astringent lotions or mild antiseptic ointment can be used several times daily.

Alternatively, take a bar of toilet soap and make a good lather – then rub your soapy hand well into the lump area; this massage, using the lather as a lubricant, will restore the circulation and help the healing process. Leave the soap on for a few minutes then dab on some surgical spirit to help harden off the area. Repeat this treatment daily until the lump has gone, and in the meantime give your horse a break from work.

Treat a fully developed gall as you would any other wound. Bathe it gently with salt water and pat dry with cotton wool. Then apply antiseptic wound powder. Keep the saddle off – you could exercise him in hand – until the wound has healed. When you next tack up place a cotton wool pad over the area. Surgical spirit can be used to harden the skin once healed.

Make a habit of feeling around the girth area with your fingers when you groom, particularly after a long ride.

· BACK PROBLEMS ·

Pressure sores and back lesions in the saddle area are very common among long distance horses. They are caused by unbalanced riding and ill-fitting saddles. If soreness is discovered the rider can minimise a deterioration in the condition by riding with his weight further forward, using the stirrups and knees to take the weight.

Saddle sores are also caused by an ill-fitting or dirty saddle, or by a loose girth which allows the saddle to move about. Pressure caused by lumps in the saddle can restrict the blood supply and in bad cases this can lead to body tissue dying, wounds opening and infection setting in. If you feel the beginning of a sore, rest the horse's back until it has disappeared.

Treat them in the same way as girth galls. If the sore is so bad that the skin is broken, the wound must be dressed with wound powder and the period of rest will need to be longer. Once the area has healed, harden the skin by dabbing it with salt water.

In severe cases saddle sores can become swollen and very painful. Clean the wound and dress with powder, and if it is still as bad after a couple of days call your vet because the horse may need an injection of antibiotics to combat the infection.

Do something about your saddle! Clean it thoroughly and if it doesn't fit the horse properly, have a saddler check it over. Once a horse has had a sore it will always be susceptible.

· MOUTH SORES ·

These can result from heavy hands and a strong horse, so that the delicate tissues at the corners of the mouth are rubbed and even split. Again rest is a good cure, but healing may be speeded up by applying salt water to the corners of the mouth. Check that the bit fits comfortably before you start work again.

VETERINARY FIRST AID
. FEET ·

Bruising or penetration of the sole can happen anywhere. Your horse may suddenly go lame – you have a look and may discover a nail or piece of wire stuck into the sole of the foot. Do *not* remove it until you have assessed the angle at which it has entered, and have found a suitable tool to remove it with – a pair of pliers or pincers. Then, grasp it firmly and give a straight, hard pull to get it out, don't ease it from side to side as this could result in the object being broken off within the foot. Keep the offending object as it will give you an idea of how deep the penetration was and of the damage that might have been caused inside the foot.

Covering the hole with powder or ointment will have no effect as the horn of the sole is a cork-like substance which closes up almost as soon as the object is removed.

The horse may make an immediate recovery, but lead him for a while before mounting up, until you are sure that he is sound.

If he is still lame, get a vet to come out to the horse, and he should see any puncture which penetrates the central third of the foot. If this is the case it may be better to leave the sharp object where it is until he arrives so that he can better assess whether any of the important structures below the sole have been damaged, and will know if an X-ray is necessary.

Lack of attention to your horse's shoes could result in a pricked sole. A worn shoe can work loose and twist sideways so that the nails on one side are forced into the sole of the foot when the horse bears his weight on it. Remove the shoe, and treat as with other penetration wounds.

For any puncture wound it is recommended that you thoroughly clean the foot with plenty of water and poultice it. This will keep the foot clean and draw out any infection; it will also help soften the sole for any paring which may be necessary. Put the foot into a bucket of warm antiseptic solution and soften and disinfect the horn before applying the poultice. Soak a piece of poultice in hot water and bandage it over the site of the penetration; enclose this with a plastic bag, then a further bandage and wrap the whole bundle up in an old sack or thick fertiliser bag. A poultice like this must be changed twice a day at least. All nails and objects from the ground are dirty and a potential source of tetanus, so you should ensure that your horse is well covered by the appropriate vaccination. If he is not, your vet will need to give him a fast-acting anti-serum which will provide immediate protection.

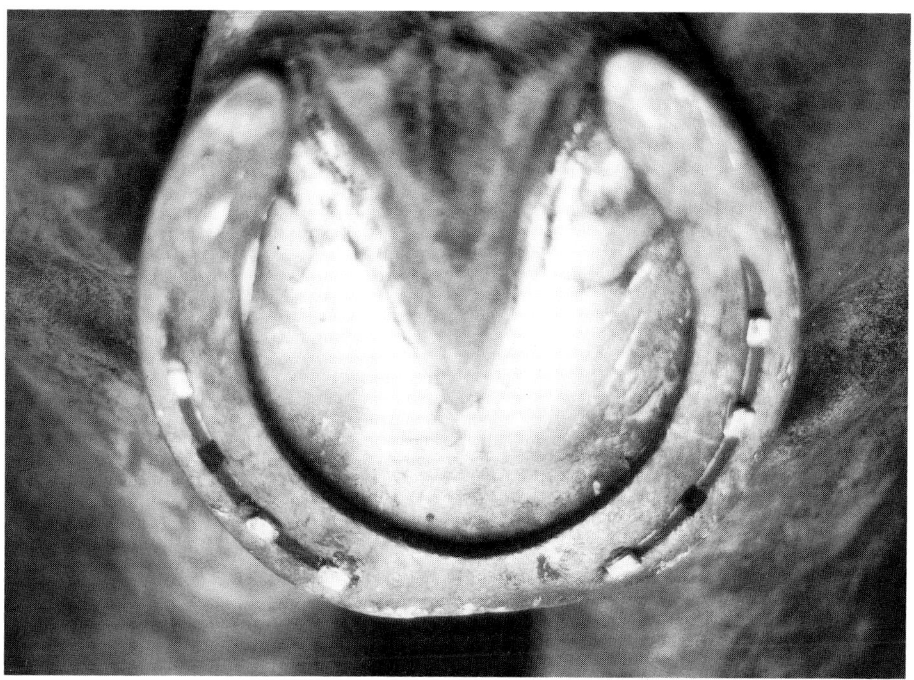

A wide web shoe (H. Price)

FEET AND SHOEING

A good farrier and comfortable shoes are vital for a horse which is to be ridden in long distance competitions. The horse works hard over a variety of terrain and no other sport has this kind of pressure on the feet over such a length of time.

Your farrier should have first class qualifications so that you know he has the best skills and knowledge. You will want to discuss any problems, and he should not be afraid to point out likely dangers, or offer new solutions. By law he is not meant to diagnose a problem (that is for the vet to do) but *do* ask his opinion – after all, he should know all there is to know about feet.

Inevitably there are fads and fashions, with varying opinions on the types of shoes to use and the methods of remedial shoeing. One farrier's methods will not be another's, but hopefully, you will reach the right solution for your horse with the local farrier.

The most commonly used shoe is the concave fullered shoe – the fullered groove provides a good grip on a variety of terrain. However, plain shoes with a wide web are very useful for long distance horses because they spread the weight and ease the pressure on the sole.

The much lighter aluminium shoe is an alternative for rides with a greater proportion of road work.

There is a variety of different irons and materials available now and a good farrier should be willing to find the most suitable shoes for your horse's particular needs.

· FEET ·

A long distance horse has to cope with a vast variety of rigorous terrain, and his feet will have a tough time. All in the same day they can be faced with heavy mud, stony tracks and boggy ground, and this can present problems for the owner and farrier who must decide how best to have the horse shod.

A good foot will have good basic conformation: a good angle from the coronary band to the toe, a good arch of sole, a well proportioned frog, strong horn and healthy coronary band. Each foot should match the rest and be balanced without tipping more weight on one side. (A foot may be larger or smaller than its partner as a result of disease or injury.)

Good foot conformation is related to the conformation of the rest of the horse, and to the angle of the pastern in particular. An upright pastern tends to produce a boxy foot, and a long, low-angled pastern will often result in a flat foot with a long toe.

Balanced action can also make all the difference when it comes to feet.

Breeding is also influential: Arabs tend to have small, boxy feet, Thoroughbreds have flat feet and sensitive soles.

Boxy feet provide too small a weight-bearing area and the foot is more prone to disease. An over-large foot will make the horse clumsy.

The ideal is a foot which is short at the toe, and deep and open at the heels so that the mechanics of the foot can function properly. It is important that the sole is thick, so that it will stand up to rough going – flat or dropped soles are easily bruised and could be a source of constant problems. The sole of the fore feet should be concave, and the hind feet even more so.

The anti-concussion device of the foot is the frog, which needs to be large and well formed. It also helps the horse 'grip' – a small or shrivelled frog will not make contact with the ground and will therefore be unable to prevent slipping.

As much as good conformation can help the horse achieve the owner's goals, so can good feet. But a horse with failings in this department should not necessarily be deemed unsuitable. Good care and good farriery can overcome most problems and the horse may eventually be able to do just as well as his better endowed companions. But it must also be said that many foot problems are related to bad farriery. So beware.

· CARE OF THE FEET ·

It is up to the owner to keep a regular check on the horse's feet, picking them out twice a day and checking the shoes and clenches; foot care should continue throughout the year, no matter what the season.

A good balanced diet will contain everything that the hoof needs for healthy growth. Biotin, a B-group vitamin, is a useful supplement as it is said to promote healthier horn growth and stimulate the keratinisation process (the hardening of the wall). A daily teaspoon of gelatine added to the feed has also been known to improve horn quality.

Obviously, because the hoof grows slowly one cannot expect to see instant results. The rate of growth depends on the individual, his age and condition, shelter and feed. On average it takes twelve months for the hoof to grow from the coronary band down to the toe. It grows evenly all around the coronary band at a rate of an inch in three months.

Cornucrescine is a dressing which acts as a mild blister; when rubbed well into the coronary band it increases the blood supply to the area and promotes hoof growth.

Changes in the condition of the horse show up in the hoof wall as rings or ridges; these relate to the food intake and reflect a change in diet, or in the quality of grass, and each foot should have corresponding rings. Hoof colour is no indication of their strength – white is no weaker than black or brown.

For the horse's feet to be healthy and function well a constant moisture level should be maintained. The hoof wall, sole and frog each contain a significant percentage of water. A certain amount is lost through evaporation, and this is replaced from within, together with a small percentage of moisture which can be absorbed through the horn. However, excessively damp conditions, marshy ground for example, may cause soft, crumbly feet.

The type of bedding can also have an adverse effect on the moisture level of the foot. For instance, sawdust balls up under the foot and draws moisture out, and when the level drops too much the wall skin will crack, resulting in brittle feet. The horse will benefit from having his feet soaked in water because this will soften up the hoof wall. Coating with an oil substance while the feet are still wet will help to seal in the moisture and prevent evaporation.

Specific foot problems may require the attention of both the vet and farrier, your vet advising, for example, on a better diet to help the feet, the farrier shoeing accordingly.

· REMEDIAL SHOEING ·

Remedial shoeing is unlimited. Whatever the problem, be it injury or conformational defect, a farrier can probably solve it.

The tendons in the foreleg are subject to great stress – lengthening the shoe can help spread the impact of each step, and give more support to the back of the leg.

Problems such as brushing and over-reaching can be solved by properly balancing the foot according to the horse's conformation and to the way the animal places his foot. Once the appropriate shoe is fitted the problem usually disappears.

Brushing is usually caused by an imbalance. One solution is to fit a feathered shoe, where the inner edge is reduced in width and fitted close in under the wall. This reduces the risk of injury if the foot does collide with the opposite leg. Another solution is to build up the weaker side, giving the inside edge a wider branch to even up the weight factor – in some cases this may be up to a quarter of an inch. The farrier should finish it in such a way that it does not catch the other leg.

Over-reaching is an injury usually to the heel area of the front leg caused by the toe of the hind foot. The solution is to modify the shoes on the fore feet so as to quicken the gait and therefore keep the heels away from the hind feet. This is done by lengthening

A shoe fitted with stud nails (H. Price

the heels to give support to the back of the leg, and rolling the toes.

However, rolled toes on the hind shoes which can also be set back and bevelled off will not cure over-reaching because they will encourage a quicker gait behind, too, and the foot has more metal at the front to catch the fore-leg. If the hind feet are fitted with rolled toes, for whatever reason, the front shoes should have rolled toes fitted to match. Toe clips can be replaced with quarter clips to allow for rolling.

· HOOF PADS ·

Not all long distance riding organisations permit the use of pads in their rides. They are used to protect feet which have suffered problems, for instance puncture wounds or shallow, soft soles. The pads will protect the sole and frog from rocky surfaces which cause bruises, and they may also absorb some of the concussion as the foot meets the ground.

However, the horse does become less sensitive to stony ground, making him more likely to wrench a shoe; and his ability to grip may be reduced since the frog is covered.

The disadvantages of pads may outweigh the advantages. There may be problems in ensuring that they fit properly and that the nails are driven high enough. If the horse has poor feet with a crumbling hoof wall, it is usually far better not to use pads unless the nails can be placed higher up.

They can be a source of further problems because they allow grit and small stones inside which will rub. And because pads do slightly alter the horse's gait, there is a greater risk of a shoe being pulled off, and the pad can cause part of the foot to be torn away, too.

Packing, ie putting a filling between the foot and the pad, will help to prevent objects working their way in.

With prolonged use the sole and frog are likely to become soft and therefore more liable to bruising when the pads are removed.

Concussion pads also offer protection for damaged or sensitive feet, and reduce the concussion to feet and legs. A cushioning material is fitted between the foot and shoe. It is shoe-shaped and leaves the frog uncovered. They also increase the amount of surface area in contact with the ground, so giving the horse a more natural feel.

Pads are permitted by both BHS and EHPS rules; however, EHPS rules accept them for completion and mileage only, and no gradings or trophy points can be achieved.

STUDS

Studs can obviously be a great advantage in difficult going where extra grip is needed. But, by fitting a single stud on the outside, there is a risk that the foot will be unbalanced and the leg damaged as a result. Studs should therefore be used in pairs on the latter quarter of the shoes, towards the heels. Many people use the large mushroom type studs but beware brushing on the hind legs with these. Other riders now prefer the stud nails which are equally as effective but less likely to cause damage.

FIRST AID

Shoeing is one instance where the need for first aid can and ought to be prevented. The horse should have been shod before a ride, and given enough time to wear the shoes in but not so much that the shoes are not still in good condition, and the nails firmly holding the shoes in place. This might be a week to ten days before the ride, so there should be little opportunity for the shoe to be loosened on the ride, whatever the terrain conditions.

If the shoe does become loose, get off and check it, and if it will cause serious problems, ask a passing rider to get the farrier to come to your assistance. You should have a spare set of shoes in your back-up vehicle. However, if the incident threatens to jeopardise a successful finish, you or your crew may be able to solve the situation yourselves; although this is *not* really advisable since you could do more harm than good.

8 Tack and Tack Care

A comfortable saddle for a hard day's riding (Jon Parslow)

One of the advantages of long distance riding is that no specialist tack is needed initially and your own general purpose saddle will be perfectly adequate. Specialist saddles and bridles are available but there is little point in buying them unless you have decided to dedicate yourself to the sport.

However, it is advisable to have a review of your current tack. Have a look at your saddle. Does it really fit as well as it could? Does it need re-stuffing, does it dip or have bumps underneath? What is the stitching like? Comfort for the horse and, indeed, the rider is of prime importance. Any bumps or ridges which could push into the horse can really do harm after several hours of riding, so sort out any potential problems before you start.

The pommel should be high enough to give the withers a good clearance, but it should not be too wide, or the gullet will drop down and put pressure on the spine, nor too narrow, or the saddle will sit too high – with the rider's position also being affected, the saddle will pinch the top of the shoulders and side of the withers. You should be able to fit your hand under the arch with someone in the saddle while you do so, providing they are of similar weight. A good practice is to have your

(page 119) A long-distance saddle with extended panels, together with a cotton-type numnah (Bob Langrish)

saddle checked yearly by a qualified saddler who should test the tree and check the stitching, and re-stuff if necessary.

When you buy a saddle make absolutely sure that you have bought the correct width for your horse's back; it must not press on the spine or pinch the skin. If you have a horse with a narrow back and high wither, a wide fitting saddle will cause concussion on his back. With long distance riding any slight defect will have exaggerated consequences.

When buying a saddle the best thing to do is have the saddler come out with a selection of widths to try on the horse. If you are having the saddle specially made, he will probably take a profile of the horse's back, measuring it length- and widthways.

If *you* have to send the measurements away to the manufacturers, measure the horse's back using a draughtsman's flexible curve, available from stationers and office suppliers. Alternatively saddlery retailers will lend you a gauge, or you could order one from the Society of Master Saddlers. Failing that, use a soft wire coat-hanger, bent over the horse's back just behind the withers, then trace the outline onto a piece of paper. You may also be asked to measure the circumference of the horse (barrel) at the pommel position, via the brisket.

Your saddle must allow complete freedom of the shoulder blades so that the horse can extend without restriction. Check that all weight is borne on the spring of the ribs, not on the spine or loins. If you are at all unsure, have a saddler come and look at the saddle on your horse – the cost will be well worth it since you could save your horse discomfort and injury, and yourself disappointment.

You may need to reconsider which bit to use as you progress but whatever you choose it must be in good condition and not thin or worn, otherwise it could pinch. By and large, an ordinary snaffle bridle, providing the leather and stitching are in good condition, will be fine.

SPECIALIST TACK

The saddles and bridles made specifically for long distance riding are designed to promote comfort in every respect. Long distance saddles are lightweight in construction which helps to reduce horse fatigue. Some are available ready-made in a selection of widths, others are made to measure. They usually have extended panels which are formed in either a fan or spur shape. The design ensures that the weight of the rider is dispersed across the maximum possible area so that the risk of pressure sores is reduced. But beware of extended panels if your horse has a short back because the saddle pressure might affect his internal organs.

Knee rolls are usually moulded, and flaps are cut relatively straight which ensures that the horse's shoulder muscles are not restricted. Both features combine to keep the rider's leg in the correct 'long' position.

The long distance saddle should have little padding to allow the rider's leg to be in close contact with the horse. This is important since a feel for the way the horse is going is so vital.

Girth straps are often strengthened with raw hide which is very much stronger than normal leather. Some long distance saddles have longer, dressage-style girth straps to avoid giving the rider sore inside legs often caused by pressure from ordinary girth straps. They have wider seats, often with a little more padding, and a higher cantle, and should incorporate a cut back pommel which eliminates pressure bumps on the withers; also a generously high gullet for maximum airflow to allow heat from the back to disperse.

The stirrup bar can be made about an inch longer which will place the leathers in a better position, particularly if the rider spends some time in a semi-standing position – otherwise you may get too far forward of the horse's centre of motion. The stirrup bars can be set outwards to minimise the risk of them bearing onto the horse's back. Stirrup leathers can be positioned below the saddle flap to prevent the leg being chafed by the leathers. Extras include plenty of 'D' rings for attaching breastplates, cruppers, saddle bags, sponges and so on.

The stuffing in your saddle should be hard enough to help keep the saddle, and the rider, in their correct positions. Soft stuffing allows the saddle to move about slightly and hill work especially will accentuate this problem and cause rubs and galls. As the horse becomes fit his shape changes, so your saddler may have to come and top up the stuffing accordingly.

Both rigid and spring trees are used in long distance saddles. The rigid tree, often viewed as old fashioned, has a greater weight-bearing surface and is stronger in construction; it seems less susceptible to metal fatigue. Spring trees are a little more comfortable for the rider.

Some riders in Britain use a synthetic saddle which is general purpose in style, with seat and flaps made of a lightweight, hard-wearing rubber-type material, and with a dressage-style girth. This all helps to put the rider in close contact with the horse.

BRIDLES

A bridle needs to be kept as simple as possible because your enemy will be any form of rubbing. So, the minimum straps and buckles is the ideal, and many do without a noseband.

Correct fitting is essential. Take care that the noseband and throatlash

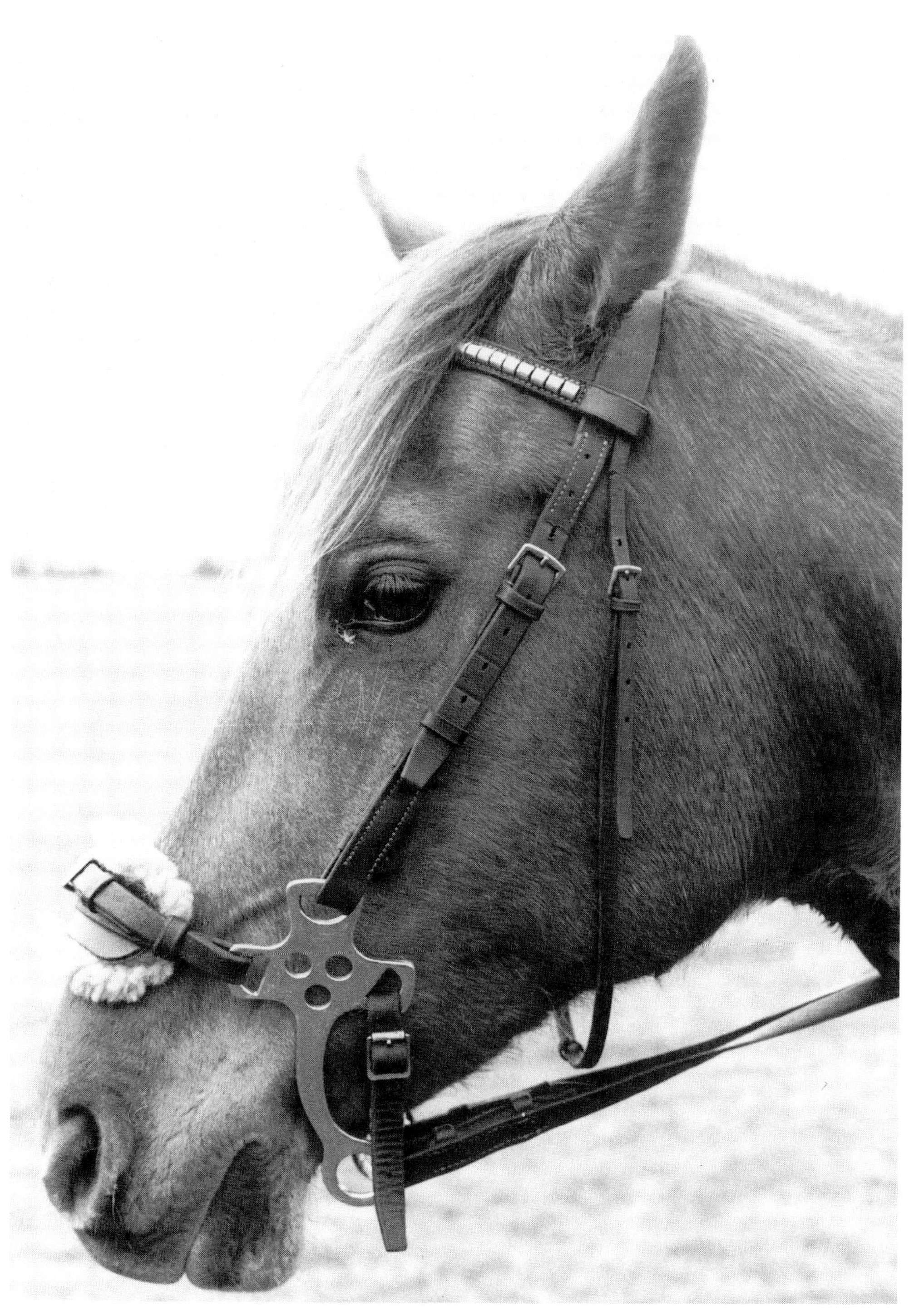

A typical hackamore bitless bridle. Care should be taken not to fit the noseband too low (Steve Moore)

are not tight. The noseband should be loose enough for you to fit two fingers between it and the horse's face. If the horse must wear a corrective noseband (drop, flash or grackle) the rider *must* reach a compromise between control and comfort for the horse. The throatlash should be fitted so that there is room for a hand's width at right angles to the horse's jaw bone.

If fitted too loose the bridle will chafe, and the bit will be incorrectly placed. The headpiece should lie flat behind the ears and hang parallel just behind the projecting cheek bones. The browband should be short enough to prevent the headband from slipping back down the neck, but long enough to avoid chafing at the base of the ears.

Bits should be fairly thick; thin bits can cause injury which will affect performance and could attract penalties. Whatever type of bit is chosen, it should fit the mouth properly, and be adequate for control; pressure and pulling will show up as bruising or lesions on the bars of the mouth.

· BITLESS BRIDLES ·

Bitless bridles avoid the problem of bit injuries, and allow the horse to drink without sucking in air and to pick at grass without having the bridle removed. Other reasons for choosing a hackamore might be horse control together with the avoidance of risking mouth sores. Most people go for the conventional hackamore with a padded noseband, which is attached to the cheek pieces of an ordinary bridle and consists of the padded noseband front, the back strap and two metal shanks. This type is the most commonly used and is known as the 'Blairs pattern'. The type with long metal shanks is a 'German' hackamore.

The front of the noseband should be padded with sheepskin; so should the backstrap, although this can be made of soft leather and is occasionally in the form of a curb chain. The bitless bridle works by putting pressure on the nose, the back of the jaw and the poll. The greater the length of the shanks, the greater the degree of leverage and the more severe the effect. It should *only* be used by those with 'light hands', and the rider may need to put more emphasis on seat, back and leg aids.

It is essential that the noseband is fitted correctly. The most common mistake is to fit the noseband too low so that it interferes with the horse's breathing. The height of the noseband should be changed occasionally to prevent callouses forming.

PAGE 125: There's no better way to see the beauty of the countryside than from the back of a horse. (below) David Abercombie and Balou with Ann Chapman and Dark Flight on one of Exmoor's stony tracks (Bob Langrish)
PAGES 126-7: A chance for a breather for horses and riders on the Golden Horseshoe Ride (Bob Langrish)

148
147

RIDING MAGAZINE
16
RIDING MAGAZINE
11

· *LDR BRIDLES* ·

There are specialist bridles on the market made of rolled leather which reduces the risk of chafing. The bit can be removed easily to convert the bridle to a head collar, ideal for drinking and management at halts. One can also buy webbing bridles which are soft yet strong and have the unique advantage of being machine washable.

OTHER EQUIPMENT

· *NUMNAHS* ·

A numnah should only be used to provide cushioning, and never to compensate for a badly fitting saddle. It should be pulled well up into the gullet so as not to block off the important air channel over the back. Care must be taken that the numnah itself does not rub the back.

If you must use one, choose natural fibres which will not 'draw' as some synthetics do – look for the padded polyester-filled type with a cotton outer. It should be larger than the saddle so that you have approximately 2.5cm to spare around the saddle's entire outline. This type of numnah does not wrinkle up and is machine washable. Have two, or perhaps three, so that you can change for a fresh one on the half-way halt of a long ride.

Some riders favour the Western-style saddle blanket which is folded into four under the saddle. The great advantage of this is that it can be re-folded during a ride to provide the horse with a fresh, clean side, up to three times. The woollen material absorbs sweat and does not slip.

The numnah to avoid is the 'tea towel' type and anything made of nylon, which won't absorb sweat and tends to wrinkle and bunch up under the saddle.

· *GIRTHS* ·

In choosing a girth your aim must be to prevent chafing and girth galls. Most suitable are the padded sort with soft, absorbent cotton lining which will absorb sweat. String girths (non-nylon) are also good because they allow air to circulate and so help prevent chafing.

Galls appear as small, hard lumps behind the horse's elbow. If ignored the hair will eventually be rubbed away leaving the skin bald, and sooner or later be rubbed raw, and will take some time to heal.

Galls are caused by pressure, pinching or friction; you could try

PAGE 128: Tackling a steep hill on Exmoor (Bob Langrish). (below) Long distance riding is the most social of all equestrian sports and provides the opportunity for riders to make lots of friends (Steve Moore – courtesy Your Horse*)*

another girth but prevention is better than cure, and cleanliness will help – clean or wash your girth regularly, and when grooming take extra care to remove dirt or dried sweat from the girth area. Use your fingers to check that there are no hidden lumps.

Girth sleeves made of cotton or sheepskin are a good idea for horses with sensitive skin, but make sure that they don't ruck up and cause the problems that they are supposed to prevent.

Girths should be neither too short nor too long. When tightened for mounting up, the buckles should reach at least to the second hole on each side and there should be at least two spare holes above the buckles on each side.

For longer competitions you will need two or three girths of the same type as it will be necessary to swap for a fresh, clean one at the half-way halt.

· BREASTPLATES ·

A breastplate prevents the saddle slipping back when riding up steep hills, and even the best fitting saddle will do this if the going is steep enough. There are two types, the English hunting type and the Western breastplate. The former consists of a neck strap attached to the front Ds of the saddle either side of the wither, and to the girth between the forelegs. Look out for one with rounded leather at the wither straps as this will help prevent chafing.

The breastplate must fit properly. You should be able to fit a hand's width at right-angles to the withers, and when in its proper position the straps joined to the Ds and to the girth should lie flat, without strain. Attachments for the running martingale should be added to the breastplate.

Western breastplates have a slight 'V' at the chest and are contoured to the horse's shape. If your horse's conformation is such that the saddle slips back easily even on the flat, a Western breastplate with a sheepskin lining is advisable.

· MARTINGALES ·

A running martingale is recommended if your horse is excitable and throws his head up. For correct fit, attach the martingale to the girth and the rings should reach to the withers. The neck strap should be loose enough to slip a hand's width at the withers, and the buckle should be at the near side. In the UK, BHS rules say that standing martingales may only be attached to cavesson nosebands.

· BOOTS ·

Boots and bandages are permitted in BHS rides, but they must be removed for veterinary inspections or on the request of the steward. Do check what is allowed, as some rides do not permit brushing boots.

If your horse brushes badly he is unsuitable for long distancing. Minor brushing can be remedied by your blacksmith and may even wear off as the horse muscles up in training.

Brushing boots do, however, collect mud or pieces of grit which may rub the skin, and cost you penalties; much the same applies to over-reach boots.

TACK CARE

To survive the ravages of wear and weather, tack needs to be properly cared for. New saddlery needs an initial treatment if it is to last and give you the service you expect, and all leather needs to be 'fed' regularly with oils to keep it supple and pliable. For the initial oiling brush a proprietary brand of saddle oil or dressing into all areas of the saddle

A version of a 'caged' stirrup which, according to BHS and EHPS rules, allows the rider to use footwear other than riding or jodhpur boots (Jon Parslow)

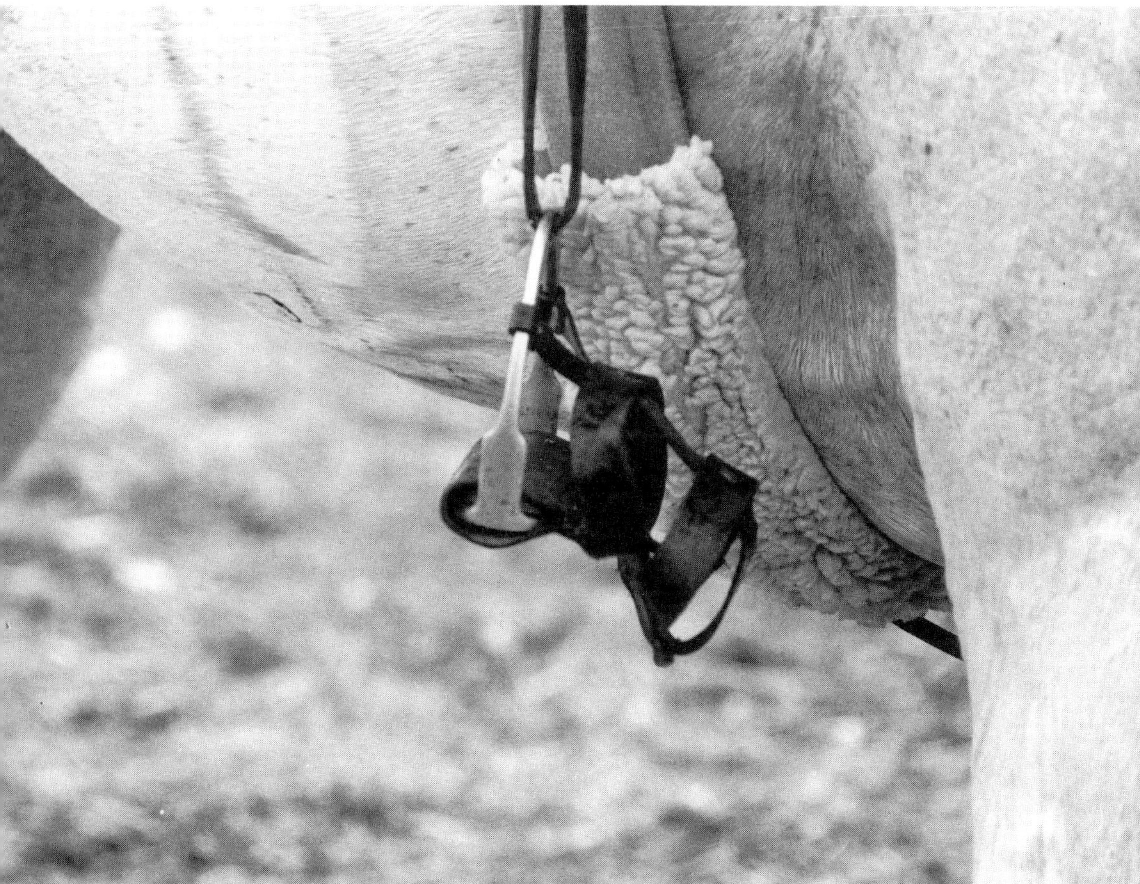

(except suede). Leave it to soak this dressing in, at room temperature; repeat the dressing again the following day. Then wipe over with a clean, dust-free-type cloth and leave for up to 48 hours, again at room temperature. Seal the oil in with glycerine saddle soap which will also help to protect the saddle from rain.

Ideally, all leather equipment should be cleaned after every ride. This is a must before and after a competitive ride. Take each item apart completely and give it a thorough clean with a good saddle soap. Neglected tack often dries out and breaks under stress – a broken stirrup leather or rein could spell disaster. If your tack gets very wet, it will need additional care; there are a number of products on the market which will help to revitalise the leather and weatherproof it.

Be sure to wash and rinse the numnah and girth thoroughly – a padded fabric-type girth could accompany the numnah into the washing machine, but choose a detergent which is not likely to irritate the horse's skin.

Inspect your tack thoroughly in these sessions, particularly before a competition; if any repairs are needed you will have plenty of time to take them along to the saddler. Stitching should be renewed at the first sign of deterioration. Also, check the bit for wear in the joints – if they become thin they will be sharp in the horse's mouth.

Tack may be inspected before the start of a ride, and if the steward decides any part of your tack is ill-fitting, unsafe or likely to cause damage to the horse, you will be asked to alter or replace it. Your horse may then be subject to additional tack inspections during the ride.

If you have to store your saddlery for any length of time be sure to clean it thoroughly, then rub a layer of petroleum jelly onto it. This will help to keep it supple and in good shape.

9 Travelling

Once you enter the more important rides you are likely to find that you are driving equally long distances. If your horse is unused to travelling, get in some practice well in advance. If he dislikes loading, spend some time persuading him that the horsebox or trailer is not such a bad place to be. Offer him his feed in it on a daily basis until he is relaxed and will walk up the ramp and stand quietly. Occasionally load him up and take him for a short drive, perhaps to the start of a good bridleway or byway, so he will associate the trailer or box with an interesting outing.

TRAILER OR HORSEBOX?

Ideally, a horsebox or lorry is always the better choice for the horse, though most people compromise with a trailer.

· *HORSEBOX OWNERSHIP* ·

The advantages of owning a horsebox are many: there is the luxury of having somewhere to brew a cup of tea, and change out of rain-soaked jodhpurs; plenty of room to store tack and rugs, and somewhere to stay – free! – where you can be close to your horse overnight. The horse has a steadier, more comfortable ride with a little more space about him. A bad loader is usually far more co-operative when faced with a ramp into the larger and more open space of a lorry.

There are also disadvantages: your lorry can be used for little else except horse transportation and the costs are higher. Your helper or crew will need separate transport. It is just impractical to follow the ride along narrow, winding lanes in a lorry – far more convenient to unhitch the towing vehicle from the trailer and use that. And when you are not using your horsebox, you do need somewhere to keep it, preferably under cover. With theft and vandalism on the increase, it also needs to be secure.

You don't need any special training to drive an ordinary-sized horsebox (accommodating up to four horses). However, anything over 7.5 ton (gross) requires a Heavy Goods Vehicle licence and a course of training with a minimum number of lessons (the approximate cost is £400).

Horseboxes are fairly easy to drive once you have become accustomed to the extra weight and width. Reversing is much easier with a horsebox. Most people are self-taught, though they may have had the benefit of an experienced horsebox driver to sit beside them on one or two journeys.

(page 133) A double front-unload trailer ready to transport horses, with a good depth of straw and hay nets ready for the journey (Steve Moore)

Good driving involves simple common sense and plenty of consideration for the horse on board. You should always read the road ahead, anticipating and braking gradually for junctions and corners, using the gear-box smoothly.

The horsebox will, of course, need separate insurance. Normally an insurance company takes into account the fact that the vehicle will not be used a great deal, and that it is used in leisure hours, so the bill is usually no more than insuring a medium to large car 'fully comprehensive' for a year (though it will be more if the driver is under 25 years).

In Britain, the MOT test for lorries is stringent so the vehicle needs to be kept well maintained through the year. To be presented for a test the vehicle must be steam cleaned underneath and around the engine, because otherwise the examiners at the Government Test Centre will not even look at it. This costs £30 to £40; the charge for the MOT, at the time of writing, is £25.

MOT testing is sometimes known as plating, which is misleading. In fact, the vehicle's 'plate' is usually to be found in the cab and gives the details of axle weight, year of manufacture, the year it was first registered and so on. This stays permanently with the vehicle and does not change with the MOT.

Road tax is the same as that taken out for a car. However, if you use your horsebox as part of a business venture, for instance charging to take other people's horses to and from events, then it would be taxed as a goods vehicle.

Fuel consumption is high, at around 16 to 20 miles (25.6km – 32km) to the gallon (4.5l) for a diesel engine (depending on the weight carried), and 12 to 14 miles (19km–22km) to the gallon for petrol.

With regular maintenance, horseboxes are usually very easy to keep in good running order. However, one thing you really must do is take care of the floor, and muck out the box every time you return from a journey.

· TRAILERS ·

A trailer has several advantages: it costs less; you can hitch it up behind your current car without incurring another tax and insurance bill (your car insurance could cover your trailer on third party basis), and you can use your towing vehicle for the back-up crew once you have unloaded at the ride venue.

The disadvantages are: it is not such a steady ride for the horse; it is more difficult to reverse; and your towing vehicle will become an extension to the trailer, simply crammed with equipment. Though this is not too unpleasant at the time, if you have to take someone important out the following day, they might not be too impressed with the smell! But there's no way out of that one.

Insure your trailer on your horse insurance, so that it is covered wherever it is parked. Under your car insurance the trailer is only covered for third party. Trailer theft is becoming big business, so acquire some form of locking device for your trailer, and make a note of the chassis number and any distinguishing features in case it is ever stolen.

Whether buying a horsebox or a trailer, the best advice is to go to a reputable dealer, particularly if you are not quite sure what you are looking for. That way you have basic consumer rights, and (in Britain) you also have the Fair Trading Act behind you should there be any problem. You would have more difficulty if you were to buy privately and something went wrong.

There is a good second-hand market in both types of horse transport. The better a vehicle is cared for the longer it will last. All prices vary according to quality and type. A new trailer, front unload, will range from £1,300 to £3,500. For a horsebox, if both the chassis and body are new, you could pay anything from £15,000 up to £100,000! The price is much higher for large horseboxes which require HGV licences and have fully furnished living quarters. A non-HGV second-hand chassis with a new body might cost around £5,000.

LOADING

If your horse is difficult to load there are several different methods you could use to get him up the ramp. Load a troublesome horse in a bridle as this will give you more control. And taking a companion horse can be a great help – load the other horse first with yours following close behind, or try tempting a reluctant loader with a feed bucket, rewarding him with a mouthful or two once he has loaded.

Should this not work enlist two helpers and attach two lunge lines to the back of the trailer, one on each side. Leave them flat on the ground until the horse is standing on or near the ramp; the helpers should pick up the ends of the lunge lines and walk towards and past one another behind the horse so that the lines are crossed just above the hocks. They should then pull gradually and firmly so that the lines tighten behind the horse as he is led up the ramp. Helpers should stand behind the line of the ramp and the horse's quarters so as to be less distracting.

If you are on your own, you will have to be very organised and have everything ready for loading in advance. Allow yourself plenty of time. Back your trailer into an enclosed space, or at least with a wall or fence down one side of the ramp. If the horse is reluctant, put a headcollar on under the bridle and attach a lunge line; lead him as far up the ramp as he will go, then loop the end through the tying ring. Move back down the ramp, get behind the horse and encourage him to go in with slight pressure on the lunge line to the head collar.

Once loaded, if your horse is experienced you can probably leave him tied up while you fasten the breeching strap and raise the ramp. If he isn't, don't tie him up – he may pull back and frighten himself. If you are in any doubt, attach a lunge line to his headcollar, loop it through the tying ring and hang on to the end while fastening the breeching; if he does panic you can slacken it without letting go completely.

If your horse is a problem, it is far better to have help at hand; some horses need all your patience and calmness to help them overcome their anxiety. In general, horses become better with practice, but do try not to give your horse a bad experience as horses have long memories. One nasty incident could prove quite a setback, perhaps curtailing your ride plans.

PREPARATION

A layer of sand on the vehicle's floor underneath the straw will provide a better grip. Some horses are afraid when they hear their feet rattling on the boards so cover the ramp with straw when loading. Hang up a hay-net for each horse but make sure they are high enough, so that when empty they don't trail.

The horse can easily knock and hurt himself, so protect him by using boots and bandages. You can buy boots specially made for travelling; they should be thickly padded, and cover from below the knee to the hoof, protecting the coronet band.

Alternatively, use wool stable bandages and gamgee, working down to cover the coronet band which is always at risk of a tread, particularly behind. Over-reach boots on the front feet are an added precaution.

You ought also to use knee and hock boots. The top buckle of each should be fitted fairly tightly, just so you can insert one finger between the strap and your horse's leg. The lower strap should be loose, even on the last hole, to allow the horse to flex his legs.

Protect the tail from being rubbed against the tailboard by using a tail bandage. Be careful not to put the bandage on too tightly – for neatness you can dampen the tail, but never wet the bandage before you put it on. You might also like to use a tail guard.

If your horse is nervous and inclined to throw his head up, add a poll guard to the headcollar. You could improvise with a small square of sponge or sheepskin attached to the headcollar.

Rugging will depend on the weather and the horse. Some owners tend to 'over rug' but the horse will quickly break out into a sweat if too warmly dressed. A cotton sheet with fillet strings may be enough, with a lightweight roller to hold rug and tail guard in place.

Try to stick to the same pre-travel routine. Get ready carefully and slowly, and never fluster the horse with your own panic.

One horse in a double trailer is better placed on the offside to compensate for the slight camber on most roads. If you have a nervous traveller or a youngster, he might be happier with the central partition removed. Before you set off, do a quick check: make sure partitions, breast bars, and the ramp are secured properly; that the doors above the ramp are pinned back safely; and that tack and equipment stored on the trailer are all secured safely. Don't leave anything in the box which could fall over and upset the horse.

An older trailer coupling, hitched up and ready to be towed. Note the breakaway cable (chain) (Steve Moore)

LONG JOURNEYS

The maximum distance travelled in one day ought to be no more than 350 miles. Long journeys can cause metabolic upsets so the horse must be allowed recovery time before the start of a ride.

On reaching the ride venue, make sure the horse has plenty of clean water and hay (carry your own water supply in a water carrier). Boots and bandages should be removed and the legs rubbed vigorously to help the circulation.

If you do have to travel a great distance aim to travel the day before and stable your horse at the venue overnight. A long journey, plus a 40–50 mile ride, is too much both for horse and rider. If your horse is a bad traveller, the overnight stay will give him the chance to recover. Make a couple of 'trial runs' first if possible – some horses don't mind new surroundings at all, others fret all night. If you can take him to a friend for an overnight stay, when the time comes for a pre-ride stay, he may be less stressed.

During long journeys make arrangements to stop and check your horse every couple of hours. Some horses are reluctant to stale while in a moving vehicle, and retention of urine can lead to serious health problems. Offer your horse a drink and check his boots, bandages and rug; also see that there is plenty of ventilation in the trailer.

DRIVING AND TOWING

Thoughtful and careful driving will make things much more comfortable for the horse. Always leave plenty of time for your journey; leaving in good time will mean you can keep to a steady pace. Horses can be upset by speed, especially at the start of a journey, as it takes a while for them to settle into a good standing position.

When you are driving, imagine a person standing up in a moving bus; that way you can visualise how the horse may be reacting to the way that you are driving. Emergency braking and jerky gear changes will throw the horse forward. So, read the road ahead and plan your movements; keep your speed down so that you can stop smoothly if necessary. The trailer weight makes a big difference to braking distances, so keep more space between yourself and the next vehicle. There is no need to use high engine revs and slip the clutch when moving off as this will lead to excessive clutch wear. Balance engine power and clutch as in a hill start. When pulling out into traffic remember that your vehicle and trailer will need a larger than normal gap, and that you take longer to speed up.

A trailer coupling in parking position with electric cable neatly bound, and a security anti-theft chain fitted (Steve Moore)

Take care on bends and corners because centrifugal force will act against the trailer, pushing it back onto a straight path; in some circumstances this could result in a skid. Keep your speed down on bends braking as little as possible and only lightly using the accelerator. The trailer will follow a much tighter turn than the towing vehicle so allow for kerbs or walls (watch out for cyclists, too). When turning at a junction give yourself room by moving away from the kerb on your approach. Check your mirrors and signal well in advance. Always indicate your intentions in plenty of time for other road users.

On approaching a hill climb change to a lower gear at the bottom; otherwise you may have to change down half-way up. Similarly, use low gears when driving downhill or the brakes will heat up – if they get too hot there could be an eventual loss of braking power altogether. With heavy duty purpose-built towing vehicles like Land-Rovers, this is less of a problem.

High winds, high-sided vehicles or excess speed can make a trailer 'snake' from side to side; this is an alarming experience. You should gradually lift your foot from the accelerator and let the vehicle slow until the snaking stops. Allow the steering wheel to twitch slightly, but keep a straight or slightly curved path. Do *not* be tempted to brake as this could cause the trailer to jack-knife or even overturn. Nor should you attempt to counteract the snaking by steering as this again could make things worse. If your trailer starts snaking while going downhill you may have to brake, very gently, to control the speed.

Reversing with a trailer simply takes practice. Just remember right hand down and the trailer goes left; left hand down, it goes right – watch its movements in your wing mirrors. Reverse at just above ticking over speed; if the vehicle and trailer do jack-knife, stop, pull forward, and start again.

Your vehicle will be using more fuel than usual so on a long journey you will probably have to stop once or twice to fill up.

When you arrive you will probably be asked to park your vehicle and trailer off the road, usually in a field. Engage four-wheel-drive, if you have it, but before you set out across country, plan your route, particularly if it is wet and muddy. Other vehicles may have created deep ruts and you could get stuck in them. Use the highest gear possible. If you do get stuck don't rev the engine as this will spin the wheels and you will sink deeper. Up and down hills, take the straightest route possible – never drive at an angle because if the towing vehicle loses traction the trailer could jack-knife. Avoid parking uphill as you will put a great deal of strain on your vehicle as you pull away. If you find that your parked vehicle has sunk slightly, put sacks or planks under the rear wheels and ask people to push as you start up, or you may dig yourself deeper in. If you become firmly stuck, a tractor will no doubt give you a tow!

Longer journeys will probably entail quite a bit of motorway driving. Watch out for high-sided vehicles and heavy lorries overtaking, the turbulence caused can be minimised by steering slightly to the left as the overtaking vehicle is almost in line. Otherwise, drive in the centre of the left lane.

Accidents can happen, no matter how careful a driver you are, and the procedure is much the same as for any motorist. If there are casualties or damage to property (other than the vehicles) the police must be called. If no one is hurt, those involved must exchange details. If possible make a quick sketch of the scene, which will be a great help when it comes to filling in the insurance form. Do not admit liability.

The BHS has a motorway rescue scheme operating throughout the country, in which volunteers are on stand-by day and night to remove horses to safety and stables can be provided.

There is also a private rescue scheme run in conjunction with the AA/BRS, specifically for horseboxes and trailers. If the mechanics cannot fix your vehicle on the spot, it guarantees that all you get home safely.

MAINTENANCE

Minimise the chance of breakdown by having your trailer regularly serviced. Your supplier or a good garage will give the mechanics an overhaul, and check that the body-work is sound.

As soon as possible after returning from a ride, clean the trailer or lorry floor. Damp straw and manure should always be removed. A permanently damp layer of muck is the most common cause of a rotten floor, and so many people don't realise how bad their floor is until their horse has put a foot through it! So, keep your trailer floor clean and dry when not in use. Park it reversed against a wall so that rain or snow will not be driven in. (This applies even if you have a rear curtain or double doors over the ramp.) Regularly test the timber with a sharp knife. If the blade goes in easily or if you would like expert advice take the trailer to your nearest dealer. Many trailers have double floors and the same test should be done from the underside too.

Trailer floors are either coated to be resistant to moisture and urine, or constructed from special timbers or plywood. So do not replace damaged floors with ordinary plywood or boards. Any damage to rubber matting should be acted on promptly as damp will soon seep through to the wooden floor. Make sure that all fastenings are oiled and in perfect working order. You never know when you might have to bring the ramp down in a hurry, and a rusty catch could mean vital seconds lost.

British law demands that the lights and reflectors are clean and in working order; that the number plate is clean; and that tyres have a depth in the tread pattern of at least 1mm along a continuous band which measures at least three-quarters of the breadth of tread and around the entire circumference. In fact, the side walls on a trailer tyre tend to perish quicker than the tread, and it is important to check these because cracking in the side of the tyre could cause a blow-out – the last thing you want on a journey to a ride! If a trailer is not used for a long time it is best to move it from time to time to minimise perishing.

· *LIGHTS* ·

A common cause of problems is the electrical system – one of the indicators will not work or the rear lights will not come on, and it can be quite infuriating. Electrical power for the trailer comes from the towing vehicle, and the problems are often caused by dirt and water thrown up from the road onto the towing connection. The trailer's lights are also vulnerable to road spray.

So, check the trailer plug and socket at the back of the vehicle for dirt. Wipe it over with a dry, dust-free cloth and re-connect. If there is no problem here but the lights still fail to come on, trace the cables back to the lights checking especially the connection blocks. On older trailers these corrode very quickly if not covered. Also, check the bulbs and fuses. Individual circuits can be traced according to the colour of the wire. The connecting wire between the towing vehicle and the trailer has been standardised in the form of a seven-pin plug and socket; the plug can only be inserted in the socket in one position. Standard colours are as follows:

Pin 1 Nearside indicator   Yellow
Pin 2 Rear fog lamp   Blue
Pin 3 Earth   White
Pin 4 Offside indicator   Green
Pin 5 Offside tail light   Brown
Pin 6 Stop lights   Red
Pin 7 Nearside tail and   Black
      number plate light

The actual wiring of the trailer will vary if it has been made outside the UK, so check the details in your ownership manual.

Common electrical faults include loose bulbs, worn wire insulation, loose or blown fuses and faulty connections.

· BRAKES ·

Most trailers have over-run brakes. When your vehicle slows down the front of the trailer attempts to 'over-run' it. As this happens pressure works on the coupling and this in turn transfers to a linkage which applies the brakes. Drivers with braking of this type need to be careful not to brake too sharply, or the horses will have an uncomfortable ride. On other trailers the coupling has to overcome the tension of a large spring before the brakes work. On some newer trailers, braking is transferred through a hydraulically controlled piston which provides a more progressive form of braking.

Apart from regular cleaning and lubricating, the brake systems should need little attention. However, if the brakes are operated by cables rather than rods, check the cables for fraying, especially around any of the main bends or fulcrums where there will be more stress. Also, check that the handbrake and ratchet are working properly. If the rubber cover perishes, exposure to the weather will cause rust and probably failure. The stem of the handbrake should be kept greased. When the trailer is parked the handbrake should be left off to keep the mechanism free. The jockey wheel is also vulnerable to road dirt and tends to seize in its stem if not kept lubricated. Any repairs should be done by experts.

You must have a 'breakaway cable', a safety device which helps to bring the trailer to a halt if it breaks away from your vehicle while you are travelling. It consists of a steel cable attached to the trailer with a loop to go over the hitch on the towing vehicle. The cable is actually capable of activating the trailer's brakes in response to those of the towing vehicle.

· YOUR VEHICLE ·

The weight of trailer that you are permitted by law to tow will depend on your vehicle's kerb weight and on the manufacturer's recommended towing weight. This figure should be found on a plate under the bonnet of the vehicle. The manufacturer will recommend the maximum gross weight of the vehicle – including trailer and load, ie horse. Roughly speaking that tends to be one-and-a-half times the weight of the vehicle, though this may vary between manufacturers so it is best to check with them or with a dealer.

Land-Rovers are a bit different in that they can pull up to $3^1/_2$ tonnes on the road (more off-road). As a rough guide large four-wheel-drive vehicles may take up to $3^1/_2$ tonnes, smaller four-wheel-drive vehicles and larger cars can cope with anything up to 2 tonnes, but usually not more than 1,500kg.

Horse trailers can weigh up to $3^1/_2$ metric tonnes though most are a lot less than that. The average double-horse trailer weighs between 2 and $2^1/_2$ tonnes gross – manufacturers give maximum gross weight for their trailers. Your animal's weight will depend on his height and build – for example, a 13hh pony will weigh 260kg (570lb); a 14.2hh cob 400kg (880lb); and a 15.2hh small hunter-type 450kg (985lb).

It is wise to buy the largest, most powerful vehicle you can afford – 1600cc minimum – and the smallest trailer that will cope with your needs. A rear-wheel-drive vehicle is better suited to towing, though of course four-wheel-drive cars have greater traction. Also, remember that you will need plenty of room to carry all your equipment. (Incidentally, check your vehicle handbook to see if the rear tyre pressures need to be increased for towing.)

TRAVELLING CHECKLISTS

This list of necessary equipment may seem endless, but each item is important and may prove crucial to the well-being of your horse and the success of your ride. It's far better to travel with too much than find you have left vital things behind.

· *HORSE MANAGEMENT* ·

Two water buckets
Five gallon water carrier
Cooler rug
Two full haynets
Travelling rug
Travelling boots/bandages

Tail bandage and tail guard
Spare set of bandages
Grooming kit including sweat
  scraper, sponges and towels
Horses'food
Waterproof exercise sheet

· *KIT FOR OVERNIGHT STAY* ·

Stable rug and roller
Extra feed and hay
Vaccination certificate (compulsory if at race-course)
Bedding (if not provided)

· *VETERINARY* ·

Cotton wool
Gamgee
Animalintex
Antiseptic powder
Healing gel
Instant ice pack
Glucose
Electrolytes

Spare blanket
Needle and thread
Scissors
4in Elastoplast strapping
Small pack gauze
Vaseline
Fly repellent

· *RIDER* ·

Crash hat
Riding boots
Jodhpurs, plus spare pair
  for rides over 50 miles

Spare jumper
Two jackets, including waterproof
  jacket
Whip

· *TACK* ·

Saddle complete with stirrup
  leathers, girth
Spare girth, leathers

Spare bit
Headcollar
Leading rein

Bridle
Spare reins
Spare bridle

Two numnahs (if used)
Breastplate

· *PERSONAL* ·

Small pocket knife
String or twine (or dental
  floss) for quick repairs (or
  leather shoelace)
Large handkerchief or
  neckscarf (makeshift bandage)
Collapsible hoof-pick
Money for telephone

Compass
Map and container
Route instructions
Glucose sweets
Pain reliever (Aspirin,
  paracetamol etc)
Safety pins
Elasticated bandage

· *EQUIPMENT FOR CREW* ·

Map
Spare shoes
Farrier's tools including
  claw hammer and nails, rasp
First-aid kit including
  healing gel
Antiseptic powder
Cotton wool
Two bandages (exercise)
Two water buckets (one for
  drinking, one for sponging)
Water containers
Headcollar

Rugs
Cooler rug
Waterproof exercise sheet
Spare tack
Body brush
Sweat scraper
Salt
Glucose
Stethoscope
Drinks for rider
Pair of gloves
First-aid kit for rider
Fly repellent

10 Ride Diaries

RIDES

One of the great attractions about long distance riding is the chance it offers to ride in challenging and spectacular surroundings. What follows here is a brief description of a selection of rides organised by the British Horse Society Long Distance Riding Group and the Endurance Horse and Pony Society.

· BREAMORE ·

This is one of three international rides run by the EHPS, and is a 50 mile (80km) endurance race. Set in the New Forest, it is flat and fast with basically good going; long tracks are strewn with small stones, however, which can catch you out. There is some road-work; part of the route runs through the village of Martin where it is compulsory to ride at walk.

The route is the same each year, and skirts the grounds of Breamore House and goes alongside some gallops. It is not a 'spectacular' ride, but competitors do have special permission to go where riders would not normally have access.

· CLENT ·

A tough ride run in March in the West Midlands, and renowned for its hills. It has 20, 30, 40 and 50 mile BHS rides, including a Golden Horseshoe qualifier – it is certainly good preparation for Exmoor. The EHPS has a pleasure ride in this area in the spring and a CTR in the autumn.

This one has a straightforward route over bridleways and tracks with little road-work; riders find it easy to keep the speed up, despite the numerous hills.

· GOLDEN HORSESHOE ·

Perhaps the major ride in the BHS LDRG calendar, the Golden Horseshoe is a challenging 100 mile ride over two days on Exmoor. The route varies each year, and the terrain includes steep rocky tracks, moorland, narrow stony paths and small sections of peaty bog plus some road-work. The weather often presents challenges too.

The venue is always the small village of Exford, and the surrounding countryside is typical open moorland, wooded coombes, and steep hills.

(page 147) Vast amounts of water, soaked in sponges, towels and rugs, are used in an attempt to cool Foxy and bring her heart rate down ready for the final vetting (see Golden Horseshoe Diary, page158) (Bob Langrish)

· GOODWOOD ·

This is one of the toughest rides in the BHS calendar. It is an international endurance ride of 100 miles based at Goodwood House on the South Downs. It is a 'gated' ride with a massed start. It is an undulating ride with plenty of steady hills. Mostly rather stony tracks, including the South Downs Way; there is some road-work.

· RAINWORTH ·

This is an EHPS ride in Nottinghamshire with a 40 mile ER and CTR. Staged in March it is always popular and is a good ride to start the season with, as it does not present any particular difficulties. The route follows forestry tracks which are mostly sandy.

· RED DRAGON ·

The second of the EHPS' major international rides, and in 1988 it moved to Llanwrtyd Wells in 'Heart of Wales'. The 50 mile CTR provides a hard course with a mixture of open moorland, forestry and bridlepaths, with very few metalled paths – 8 mph is quite attainable.

The ER, 100 miles over two days, crosses the so-called 'Green Desert of Wales' and is a mixture of open mountain, forestry and roads. It has the reputation of being a tough ride.

· RIDGEWAY ·

A Golden Horseshoe qualifier (40 miles [64km]), this BHS ride is very popular because there is no road-work, the going is good and the tracks are not too stony. The route runs across the top of the Ridgeway for 20 miles to the west, loops back to the start/finish then goes out 20 miles to the east. The good going means that it is fairly fast – it can be ridden at trot at approximately 11mph.

· SUMMER SOLSTICE ·

A 100 mile EHPS endurance race ridden in one day, it was started in 1978 and was the first of its kind in Britain. The venue changes and the race has been run on the South Downs, Sussex, in Sherwood Forest, Nottinghamshire, and in 1988 it was held in Hexham, Northumberland.

The 1988 ride was tough, with varied terrain – moorland bridlepaths and shooting tracks, and a forestry section and quiet roads with good verges. The route was undulating but not steep and crossed numerous streams. The scenery was spectacular in places. It also featured a 30-minute compulsory gate hold for the first time.

· *THREE RIVERS RIDES* ·

This is the BHS LDRG National Championship over 100 miles. The route has a 40-mile loop with a vet gate half-way and a second 30-mile loop which has to be ridden twice. The 100-milers have a massed start at around 5am.

The route is over some of the most attractive bridleways in Wiltshire, along ox droves and through the pleasant woodland of the Great Ridge. The tracks are stony, and the old Roman road tends to be a bit 'too straight'. Salisbury race-course provides dormitory and stabling facilities. The route is marked and patrolled by West Wiltshire trail riders, who also lead the 100 and 75 milers out in the dark.

· *YORKSHIRE WOLDS* ·

This is an EHPS ride with a 50 mile CTR and a Fast 25 mile CTR. West of Hull, the 1988 route consisted of undulating terrain, quiet lanes with good verges and fast farm tracks. There were some steady climbs to give good muscle and lung training without fear of over-stretching the horses. For an experienced horse it was relatively easy and for a novice it was hard enough without being off-putting.

It was hoped to change the venue around the Yorkshire Wolds area on different years for variety.

ARAB HORSE SOCIETY MARATHON

The AHS Marathon is a race held over $26^{1}/_{4}$ miles (41.8km). Although it is organised by the breed society, it is not limited to Arabs – any breed may enter. The horse must be over 6 years and above 14.2hh and the owner must be a member of the AHS. The first marathon was run in 1974. It bears little relation to a long distance ride, since horses race continuously. The route is over natural country with a half-mile compulsory walk section at about two-thirds of the distance, to allow the vets to watch the horses as they pass. It gives horse and rider a chance to catch their breath and perhaps attain 'second wind'.

To compete the horse needs to be very fit. There is strict vetting the night before the race and horses are vetted again twenty minutes after the finish. The organisers can withhold a prize if a horse appears to be unduly distressed, though since it is not expected to turn out and do the same thing the following day, they say this is unlikely. The vetting is to protect the horse and educate the rider – the winner is the first past the post.

There is a massed start, as in a normal race; if in the future the number of entrants were to exceed the 25 to 35 norm, the race would have to divide. It does have a considerable amount of interest and to help keep the numbers down entrants must declare approximately ten days before; usually the organisers find that withdrawals leave them roughly a third of the original entry.

The record time is 1 hour 25 mins and was set on Salisbury Plain in 1978 by an Anglo Arab mare Anstey, ridden by Finn Guinness, carrying 12.5 stone. Nine years later Finn Guinness won the race riding Anstey's daughter Merelina, both mares owned and bred by Lord and Lady Moyne. The average time is 1 hour 32 mins. The minimum weight to be carried is $11^1/_2$ stone (56kg) – this is to encourage men to enter. The minimum age for the rider is 18.

The marathon has had a number of venues including Salisbury, Exmoor and the Chilterns, and until 1988 Belvoir Castle in Lincolnshire – all routes suitable for galloping.

It tends to attract riders from both racing and long distance riding; first-time competitors are encouraged to use their first marathon for experience without setting out to win.

Horses which complete the distance are awarded a commemorative rosette, and those which finish particulary well are awarded a special certificate, much coveted for premium mares and stallions.

RIDE DIARIES

The aim of this section is to give the reader a true insight into what happens on a long distance ride. First of all is the pleasure ride, as for most riders this is their introduction to the sport.

PLEASURE RIDE

Julia Hartley has been long distance riding for four years and thoroughly enjoys doing pleasure rides. She became interested in the sport having done a sponsored ride, and it was Nottinghamshire's bridleway officer who sent her in the direction of the Endurance Horse and Pony Society.

'My first pleasure ride was at Lincoln, a flat ride and very fast which I thoroughly enjoyed. Then I did the Summer Solstice Pleasure Ride and the Harlington Ride, near Doncaster.'

Julia, a member of the EHPS Nottingham Area Group, admits to being a nervous rider and believes that she was attracted to the sport because she didn't like jumping.

> I don't jump but I like riding for pleasure. I am interested in conservation and wildlife and it just seems to fit in with enjoying the countryside.
>
> One of the things about pleasure riding is that you have got time. You can

go at the speed you want, chat to people you meet, pass the time of day with check-point people. You haven't got the pressure on you and don't have to be competitive to take part in something which is properly organised.

I am not the sort to gallop around. A lot of people make a social occasion out of it – I don't mind riding with someone but I do like to look at the countryside. You see things which you wouldn't see if you were on foot.

With pleasure rides, neither you nor the horse needs to be so fit, which is ideal if you have a full-time job. It's nice to get out when you are working hard – its sets you up for the rest of the week.

Julia took a 4-year-old Dales pony mare to the Rainworth ride in Nottinghamshire, a short drive from her home. This EHPS ride is very popular among riders and its quota of 100 entrants was quickly filled. It is one of the first of the season and riders travel long distances to take part. The venue is on the edge of part of the old Sherwood Forest. The route, marked by line arrows on the ground, takes riders along sandy forest tracks, out through National Coal Board property and along harder tracks. There are gentle slopes to contend with and plenty of softer going to pick up speed on.

The organiser had instructed riders doing the pleasure ride to set out before 11.30am to ensure that no-one arrived back too late in the afternoon. A minimum speed of 5mph is given to discourage too much dawdling – in pace terms a slow trot would get you back to base at $5\frac{1}{2}$mph. A pleasure ride can therefore be ridden almost as an everyday hack, a mixture of walk, trot and canter without any great need for speed.

On arrival Julia opened the top door of the trailer to allow the pony a chance to look about her, checked that she was OK, and went off to 'check in' with the secretary and pick up her competitor number.

The pair set off into the forest at 11.09am – Julia picked up her time from a time steward who was sitting in a car at the start of the route.

I set off on my own. Several people passed us which she wasn't very happy about, but she's got to learn. I let her trot for the first half mile because she was upset when the horses came past, and to get the initial 'tickle' out of her. Cobs are different from Arabs or Thoroughbreds. They get tired and then they rest, and then are ready to go on again.

It was a lovely ride. I didn't canter much because she soon tires, so we mostly trotted. Most pleasure riders tend to go at this sort of pace – they simply enjoy riding around someone else's country. The forest tracks are lovely and there is no roadwork whatsoever on this ride.

At one point I rode alongside a girl who was doing the 25 mile; I was doing the 15 mile so eventually we had to go in different directions. Two others ahead of us had turned to go along my route, but my little mare didn't know which way to turn – she wanted to keep with the horse we'd been riding with. When I pointed her towards the other two she just shot off up the track after them!

We rode with these two for a while. They would either walk or canter. I decided to get off and walk with her for a while because I knew she was tired. I took her round and off the track a bit and waited until the others had gone out of sight.

I was on my own the rest of the way back. She was quite tired by then and didn't mind other horses passing her. We walked and trotted back towards the venue, and when she realised she was not far from 'home' she really began to slow up.

We got back at about 2.20pm. I was aiming for three hours which works out at a speed of 5mph.

Her mare was pleased to be back at base and among other horses and quickly relaxed when loaded back into her trailer and given a hay net to munch at. She'd clearly enjoyed her day.

BRONZE BUCKLE DIARY
· *A YOUNGSTER'S START* ·

Gloriant is Jane Welcher's third long distance horse. He is an ex-flat racehorse and at the time of writing was making his debut in the sport. It was all very new to him, in his five years he'd only been used to the soft grass of the gallops and race-courses.

Jane began a training regime with him in late January, early February. At first she rode him an average of five or six miles a day, mostly walking, with more miles at the weekend, perhaps around 12 miles (19km). By the end of February he was doing 12 miles at $6^1/_2$mph fairly easily. On a 15 mile (24km) ride he could trot ten miles (16km) quite happily, and by this time he was fit enough to complete 20 miles (32km) at $6^1/_2$mph. It takes some time before a horse is fit enough for speed work.

At the start of the season Jane had planned to ride him in the Rainworth 20 CTR, do a BHS Bronze Buckle qualifier, a Bronze Buckle final, a Silver Stirrup qualifier and a Silver Stirrup final. Working up to Rainworth Glori was doing around 8 to 9 miles (14km) a day, and between 12 and 15 miles (24km) at weekends, at no more than $7^1/_2$mph.

Unfortunately in the week before Rainworth, Glori suffered an abscess in a hind foot. On the ride day he was rideable and Jane took him along just for the experience. They rode a small loop of the route and Jane was very pleased by his reaction to it all.

Two weeks later at the beginning of April, she took him along to a Bronze Buckle qualifier of 20 miles (32km) organised by the East Anglian Trail Riders Association near Fakenham, Norfolk. By this time he was

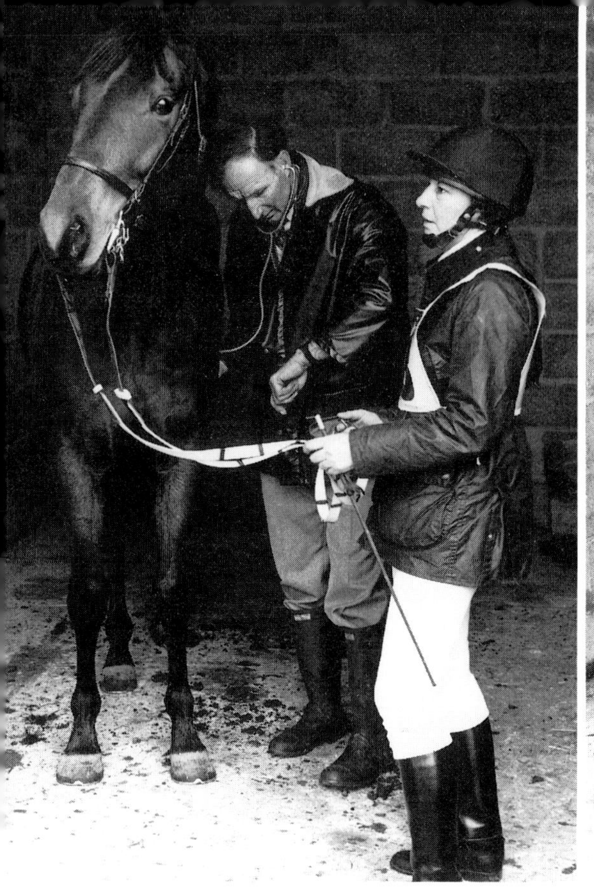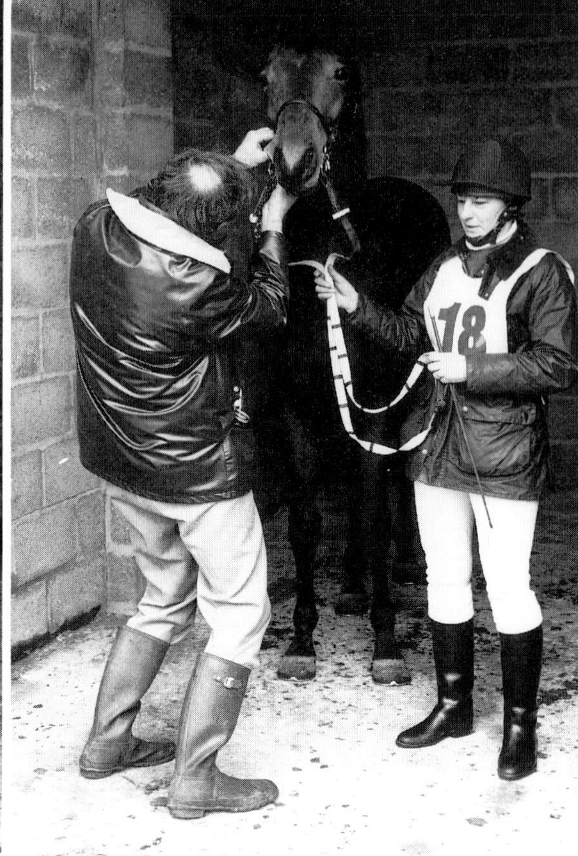

Glori has his pulse taken . . .and in the pre-ride vetting has his mouth checked by the vet (Steve Moore)

being ridden 6 or 7 miles four or five evenings a week. To successfully complete a Bronze Buckle qualifier the distance must be ridden at $6\frac{1}{2}$ mph and the horse must pass the veterinary inspections.

Jane and her friend Sally arrived in good time for their vetting time of 10.30am. Having signed in and acquired their numbers, they went back to the lorry to unload and prepare the horses for the vet and tack inspections.

Examining Glori, the vet paid particular attention to legs and feet. He called out scars and an over-reach injury so that they could be noted by his assistant. The pulse check revealed that Glori had a rate of 34, below the usual resting pulse rate of 36–45 so Jane was well pleased. Having trotted up and been pronounced sound, it was on with the saddle and over to the BHS steward for the tack inspection.

The check is to see that the tack is comfortable and safe, that it complies with regulations and does not have prohibited items such as draw reins. On completing this check, a tag with the organiser's name and phone number is attached to the saddle – if horse and rider part company, whoever finds the horse knows where it has come from and whom to contact.

Jane and Sally set off on the route at 11.15am. When picking up their numbers they had made a note of the distance between check-points and before they set out had worked out how long it should take to reach them. Sally wrote the times with a Biro on her hand. There were check-points at $3^1/_2$ miles (4.6km), 10 miles (16km) and $16^1/_2$ miles (26.5km), with the finish at $21^1/_2$ miles (34.5km).

The ride was along wide bridleways, tracks and quiet country lanes. There was a fair bit of road-work but a number of wide grassy verges saved the horses' legs and gave them a chance to canter. Some of the tracks were quite muddy – on one they were fetlock deep in water – others were fairly stony.

The route was well marked with a mixture of lime arrows on the ground and coloured tags attached to trees and posts. Colours denoted instructions 'straight on', 'turn left', and 'turn right'. The ride was set in the flat countryside of north Norfolk not far from the coast, through pretty villages with flint-stoned cottages. The weather was mild and many horses quickly sweated up.

Jane reported that Glori had thoroughly enjoyed himself; she was really pleased with the way he had reacted on his first competitive ride and had lots of praise for him on their return. They had half-an-hour to cool the horses after the ride and before the vetting. Their helper, Jane's husband Bernard, was on hand with buckets of water.

Glori's girth was loosened for a few minutes, then undone but only one girth buckle at a time to help reduce the pressure on his

Jane and Glori leaving the start on his first Bronze Medal ride (Steve Moore)

18

At the end of the ride Glori is walked round quietly, and his girth is released gradually to relieve pressure on his back slowly (Steve Moore)

back gradually. His unclipped winter coat was damp with sweat and he was lightly sponged over to help cool him down. Removing his bridle and putting on a headcollar, Jane allowed him to pick at grass around him. She then used the remaining time to walk him away from the line of boxes, to give him a chance to cool and prevent muscle stiffness setting in.

At the vet inspection Glori was found to have a pulse rate of 40 which Jane was pleased with. However, when he was trotted up he was slightly lame. On examination the vet found that the horse had a bruised sole, probably caused by a sharp stone. As the rules state that a horse should finish fit enough to complete another third of the ride, they were sadly eliminated.

GOLDEN HORSESHOE

The Golden Horseshoe is a terrifically exciting ride, and has, for many years, held the accolade of being Britain's top long distance ride. At approximately 100 miles (160km) run over two days, it is the longest. It is

Jane and Sally make the best of a grassy bridleway (Steve Moore)

held on Exmoor with its base in the small village of Exford where it has been held since 1974. Before that it was held in various other locations.

The ride has been organised by the BHS Long Distance Riding Group since 1964. There are gold, silver and bronze awards to be won: gold is awarded for a minimum average speed of 8mph (12.8kmph) each day with no vet penalties; silver for a minium average speed of 8mph with 1 to 3 penalties or a speed of 7mph with no penalties; bronze for 8 mph with 4 to 6 penalties, 7mph with 1 to 3 penalties or 6.5mph with no penalties. Rosettes are presented for 7mph with 4 to 6 penalties, and 6.5mph with 1 to 3 penalties.

To enter, competitors must have successfully completed a Golden Horseshoe qualifier ride which is over 40 miles (64km) to be ridden at a minimum average speed of 7.5mph (12kmph). At the time of writing there were eleven qualifying rides.

There is also a 50 mile (80km) ride held on the second day, and for this ride competitors must also have successfully completed a Golden Horseshoe qualifier.

The 100 mile (160km) ride is a 50 mile route used for both days, being ridden in the reverse direction on the second day. The conditions and level of difficulty vary from year to year, often depending on the weather conditions. The 1988 ride, as well as having a fairly tough route, gave the riders extra problems because warm weather had made the going hard and the heat created extra problems for the horses. Their effect was borne out by the results.

The Golden Horseshoe ride has open moorland, steep hilly climbs, tracks through forestry, wooded combes, roadwork on quiet lanes, and plenty of streams to cross.

GOLDEN HORSESHOE DIARY

Exford awakes to the fact that it's Golden Horseshoe time again in the mid-week previous to the ride when those horses and riders who have had to travel long distances begin to arrive. Of course, the organisers have been hard at work long before this, so that all that remains for them to do is to put the coloured route markers in place. The later this can be done the better since there are always vandals about to knock them over or move them – and that includes cows and sheep.

Things really begin to get under way on Sunday morning, the day before the ride. Lorries and trailers begin their descent into the village early in the morning. The ride office opens for declarations for the 100 mile ride at 8am.

It was the intention of the author to give a full ride diary of Pam

Pam works hard to persuade Foxy to trot up for the vet at the start of the Golden Horseshoe (Bob Langrish)

James's progress over the 100 mile ride. But unfortunately, the ride defeated them at the end of the first day when Forest Fox was 'spun' (eliminated) by the vet. In fact, the hot weather and tough route caused problems for many, and a number of others were spun on the first day. No gold awards were awarded, and only one silver.

Nevertheless an account of what happened on that first day will give those who have never ridden at the Golden Horseshoe an insight into what to expect.

· DIARY ·

Sunday: Pam and Forest Fox (Foxy) arrive in Exford soon after 8am. The horse was installed into a stable in a yard that Pam has always used for the ride, and Foxy has the same stable. She settled happily and was given a small feed.

Pam went down into the village to register for the ride and pick up her number and vet card. Her start time, revised because of a withdrawal, was to be a bit earlier at 8.08am. She then returned to the yard to sort things out.

2pm: Two vets and a steward arrive at the yard for the vetting and tack inspection. One took the horse's resting pulse, another looked at her lumps and bumps and saw her being trotted up. The steward checked the tack. (This was the usual routine.) Foxy's pulse rate was found to be 36/60, which was about normal for her. Pam had to point out her old scars, brushing marks etc so that they would not be picked up by the vet the next day as having been sustained during the ride. The details were noted down by the vet writer. The horse was then trotted up the road outside the yard so that the vet could see how she moved normally, so that he had a mental picture to compare with her action at the end of the ride.

For the tack inspection the steward was looking to see that the saddle and bridle were in good condition and that they fitted the horse. He cast an eye over the stitching and buckles and was quite happy with it all. Pam had Foxy in a pelham bridle with double reins because she felt that she would have better control; but she feared that if the horse did pull, she might open up old tiny cracks in the corners of her mouth. She mentioned this to the vet.

2.30pm: She set off for an hour's hack to loosen the horse up.

3.30pm: They return to the yard. Foxy was untacked and sponged lightly as she was a bit sweaty.

3.45pm: All equipment to be carried by Pam's helper was unloaded from the car, to be organised. Three water carriers were filled, and loaded so as to be easily accessible, together with three buckets and several sponges. Also placed for easy access was a bucket with grooming essentials – hoof pick, body brush, dandy brush, curry comb, sweat scraper, electrolytes and a syringe. There was a box of spare tack, including a snaffle bridle, stirrup leathers and so on, and a spare set of shoes. Two large bags contained rugs, spare girths and girth sleeves, numnahs and saddle cloths.

4.15pm: Pam cleaned her tack, including the spare bridle. The saddle and stirrup leathers were oiled, together with her French style long leather riding boots.

4.50pm: It's time for a breather. Pam drives down into Exford for coffee and a bite to eat before going to the village hall for the rider briefing. Other riders and helpers are milling about giving the little village a busy feel to it. Tourists out for the day are clearly puzzled by this activity and obviously unaware of tomorrow's exciting event.

6pm: About 80 riders and their back-up crews are crammed into the village hall. Diane Swales, the ride chairman, opened the proceedings by explaining a few of the rules, pointing out the $1/4$ mile compulsory walk section towards the end of the route each day, where a vet would be looking at the horses for signs of fatigue.

Alison Kent, the route organiser, then outlined the route explaining changes and warning about sections where riders were to take special care including boggy areas. As there were lots of gates, riders were given an extra ten minutes to allow for the time taken opening and closing them.

Crews took note of where vets and farriers were to be located en route, and where they could and could not take their cars. Two emergency phone numbers were given out.

A vet warned about the expected warm weather and the possible effects on the horses. He told riders to keep their speed down and to make sure that their horses were given plenty of opportunity to drink. The proceedings were then opened to questions.

7.45pm: The briefing ends and riders and helpers disperse to all corners of the village to their horses. Pam returned to the yard to give Foxy her feed and have dinner herself.

· MONDAY ·

6.30am: Foxy is fed and groomed, and Pam gets herself ready. She ties a sponge, specially fitted with an eyelet hole, to a D-ring at the front of the saddle. So that she can make the most of the streams and field troughs she passes, she has made a scoop out of a large orange squash bottle; this is tied on the saddle on the other side.

7.45am: Pam's helper is Rosemary Attfield, an experienced long distance rider herself, who has groomed for Pam in Rome and Germany. The night before she had marked the route onto an OS 1:25000 map and worked out the timing for Pam at 8mph, $8^{1}/_{2}$mph and 9mph. The route description gives the number of miles covered to each checkpoint, and she has marked down the time Pam should arrive at each one. Before the start Rosemary checks the contents of her car, and makes last-minute alterations. Drink and cereal bars for Pam are added to the gear.

8am: Pam rides into the start area where Rosemary is waiting for her. The car park and auction field is now abuzz with people. Riders and crews are keyed up and ready to go.

8.08am: Pam starts on the dot and sets off out of the village at a smart trot. She has already walked and trotted Foxy around the village as a warm-up. Rosemary jumps into her car and sets off for the first meeting point, Checkpoint One.

The first six miles of the route include a steep climb. A stony bridleway then takes them down to a road and Checkpoint One. Rosemary is waiting 50yds from this, ready with a bucket of water. Foxy takes a drink but, anxious to get on and keep an eye on the other horses, she manages to give Rosemary a quick shower in the process. Pam has caught up with

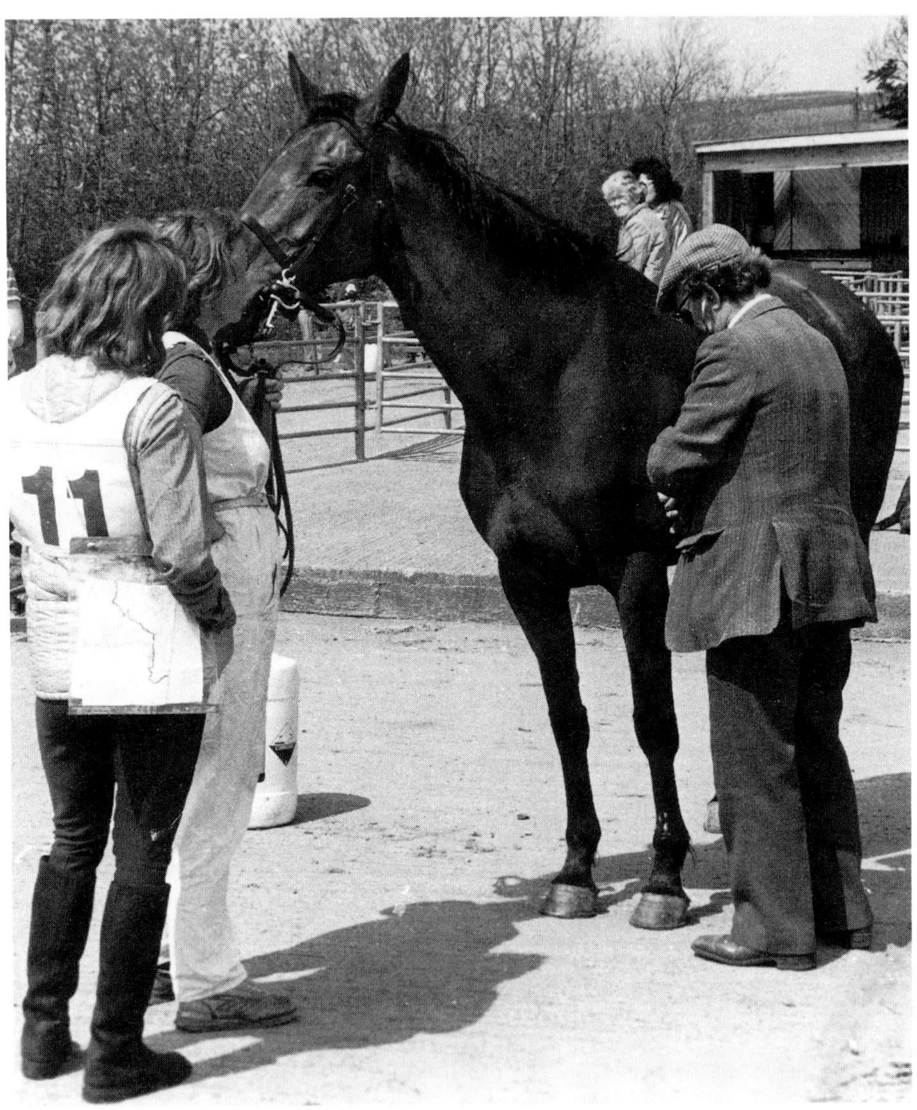

Anxious moments at the half-way halt as Foxy's pulse is taken (Bob Langrish)

another rider by now and others seem to be speeding on, though she has managed to keep to 8mph (12.8 kmph).

The route took Pam along a track, across fields, and down through a forestry plantation. Riders are guided by strategically placed flags – there's no time to consult maps or route descriptions (talk rounds). Rosemary next raced on to Checkpoint Three, missing out Checkpoint Two because it was difficult to get to in the time.

After Checkpoint Two (10 miles [16km]), more fields and a road

It's certainly thirsty work. Pam's helper provides both with refreshments on one of their many meetings en route (Bob Langrish)

to Checkpoint Three (12½ miles [20km]). The route was very much up and down, but Pam had been able to stick to 8mph and arrived at Checkpoint Three at the time she was expected.

By now Foxy and her rider were feeling the heat. The horse took a good drink and was treated to a dripping sponge down her neck. Pam managed a quick drink then sped off down the road for a fast section across moorland. The rider cannot afford to lose vital seconds, so the helper must have what is needed to hand, and supply water and drinks quickly. Rosemary met her again twice before the Half-Way Halt with more water for the horse to drink and to cool her off with.

The route to Half-Way Halt at Wheddon Cross was a little more demanding with more hills, slippery farmyard paths and stony tracks. By the time they reached the village they had completed 24½ miles (39.2km).

Rosemary had driven across the auction field, site of the halt, to a shady corner under trees just a few minutes before Pam appeared. She rode in a minute ahead of time, gave her vet card to the steward on the gate, dismounted and led Foxy across to the car.

Rosemary worked quickly to have Foxy cooled so that her pulse rate was down for the veterinary judging. The bridle was removed and replaced with a head collar and the girth was loosened for a few minutes before the saddle was removed. Foxy was offered water and allowed to pick at grass. She was given a syringe of neat electrolytes – Pam likes to know that Foxy has had them, but she only does it this way when she is absolutely sure that the horse has had plenty to drink beforehand. Otherwise it could cause a reverse osmotic effect, bad because water is actually diverted from the bloodstream to the gut.

Foxy is thoroughly sponged over until her neck and shoulders are dripping. Two long, thick sponges are soaked and placed across her neck and withers. Her legs are bathed and checked over for cuts and brushing marks. Pam has a drink and a quick bite to eat – the halt doesn't give too much time for a breather. The twenty minutes is soon up and Foxy must be vetted.

Foxy is checked by the vet for lumps and bumps before doing the timed trot up (minute test). Her pulse is OK so she's quickly taken back to the back-up car to be tacked up. Zinc and castor oil ointment is smeared on the corners of her mouth and on the edge of the bit to prevent it making the corners of her mouth sore if she were to start pulling. It is also rubbed onto her lower legs to prevent any brushing injuries.

She has a fresh girth and girth sleeve, and a clean saddle blanket. Pam takes a spray bottle she has filled with water and ties it with string around her neck, ready to spray over Foxy and herself.

Rosemary refills one of the water carriers, consults the map, and sets

Pam and Foxy cross the finish at the end of a tough day's ride (Bob Langirsh)

off for the next meeting point; there, Foxy has another drink, is sponged and Pam also drinks. (A rider can also be susceptible to dehydration.)

The tracks from here on were very stony and Pam tries as best she can to avoid them and slows down as a result. By the time she next meets her back-up she is five minutes down and is rather anxious to make up the time she has lost. At Checkpoint Six, $8\frac{1}{2}$ miles (13.6km) after the Half-Way Halt, she was still five minutes down. The going is still not very good.

Her faithful helper met her just before Checkpoint Eight. The route up until then had gone through woods, and riders ahead of her had been delayed because a number of the flags had been knocked down or moved. Valuable time was lost by the leading rider Joan Allen, who until then had been making very good time. It was now mid-day and a cool breeze was blowing up on the moors, but down in the wooded combes it was much warmer. Pam jettisoned her quilted waistcoat at this point and took a quick drink as Foxy was watered.

Rosemary met her again at Checkpoint Nine and Foxy was given more electrolytes with the syringe. They were three quarters of the way round with faster open moorland ahead where they could make up some of the time they had lost. However, they still had to negotiate more difficult paths.

At her next meeting with Rosemary, Pam was ten minutes behind time. After a very brief discussion she decided it was worth trying to make up time, to recover her 8mph average and go for gold. She completed the final nine miles across moorland at a steady canter. It was a risk because Foxy's heart rate would be pushed up but she felt that it was a risk worth taking. As a result Pam and Foxy arrived at Exford at the right time.

It was immediately a case of all hands on deck and Rosemary and Pam worked hard with water and sponges to cool Foxy down to encourage her pulse rate to drop. A check with a stethoscope proved that she was way above the accepted rate, so the cooling off operation became even more frantic. Foxy was drenched head to foot in water – the two long sponges and a light rug soaked in water were draped over her, Pam and Rosemary kept pouring water over her and so it wasn't long before the water carriers were emptied and extra supplies had to be taken from the river Exe, bucket by bucket.

All too soon the time was up, and still sponging her down, Foxy was led to the vet for the all-revealing pulse test. She was found to have a pulse rate of 70, which meant she was eliminated. Pam was very disappointed as back in the shade a minute or two before she was presented to the vet, they had found her pulse rate to be 58.

So Pam's risk had unfortunately not paid off – at the beginning of those final nine miles she could have aimed for the lower speed and a silver medal (providing they attained no penalties) but she had wanted to try for gold. She accepted her bad luck with equanimity.

Rosemary loaded all the equipment into the car and Pam led Foxy back to the yard. Once installed in her stable Foxy was checked over, groomed, given water and a small feed. The horse appeared none the worse for wear, and within ten minutes of being back in her stable her pulse rate had dropped back to about 48. A clay and mineral-based liniment was rubbed thickly onto her legs to help cool them and prevent lumps and bumps from appearing.

Foxy was given hay and rugged up for the night. Pam kept a regular check on her but she was fine. Next morning they went out for an hour's hack to loosen her up ready for her journey home.

SUMMER SOLSTICE DIARY

Egyptian Khalifa (Kelly) is an 8-year-old 15.3hh Crabbet/Egyptian Arab, chestnut gelding, owned by Jill Thomas. He has won Gold on the Golden Horseshoe, won the 70-mile gated ride on Salisbury, Bronze at Goodwood, and Bronze in the 1988 Golden Horseshoe.

The Solstice at Hexham was the furthest they had travelled for a ride (they live near Penzance). It was to be their first try at doing 100 miles in one day. They had won the class at Salisbury at 9.2mph for 70 miles so Jill was quite happy about having a go, although she was concerned about having to carry nearly a stone of lead weight and the fact that they had competed in the Golden Horseshoe Ride only a month before.

· MONDAY 20th ·

The Solstice for us started on Monday 20th, five days before the ride, with the blacksmith's visit. All Kelly's shoes are welded (or hardened) with tungsten tip nails for added grip behind. While Kelly was being shod I checked through the equipment on the list and gathered it all together in an empty stable ready for loading later in the evening. Kelly was then turned out for several hours. I had borrowed a rather large van to tow with so spent half an hour practising driving it – tomorrow I would be driving for ten hours with the trailer behind.

7pm: The trailer is hitched up and taken over to the farm where both van and trailer are loaded with all the equipment needed for the horse and two people for over a week. Kelly is then groomed and fed and his travel bandages placed ready for the morning.

· TUESDAY 21st

4am: Drive one mile to farm, feed, muck out, bandage, groom and rug up. Return home for breakfast, last minute check on flu papers, maps, money etc.

6am: Return to farm; my usual crew, David my husband, is unable to get away for long enough so he is travelling as far as Exeter where we will meet my helper for the Solstice, Wendy Dunham, a long distance rider whose own horse was to be competing at Goodwood on the same weekend with another rider. We load Kelly and leave.

9.20am: After a quiet trip we pull in at Exeter Services to find Wendy waiting. While her gear is transferred to the van I give Kelly a small feed and top up his hay net. David returns to St Just with Wendy's vehicle and we hit the motorway. Someone told me Hexham was Carlisle turn right – well, they were right! With half-an-hour's stop for lunch, we drive up the motorway all day until 4pm; when we leave the motorway, the relief at being away from heavy traffic is incredible.

4.30pm: We arrive at Liz Finney's home where we have a stable for Kelly and accommodation for us. We were very grateful for the use of a paddock where Kelly could unwind (and roll) after spending so long in the trailer. Call out the AA to change a front tyre on the van which has got a rather nasty split.

7.30pm: Settle Kelly for the night, we have a lovely meal and find a phone box to call home. Later, we fall into bed, shattered.

· WEDNESDAY 22nd ·

8am: Feed, have breakfast, muck out, bandage. Make a check to make sure we have everything, and an hour later we are hitting the motorway for another day's driving.

2.15pm: Arrive at Hexham! After having the flu papers checked and finding out the stable number, we unload Kelly and let him stretch his legs for half-an-hour or so. During the afternoon, we settle in – erect our tent and put up beds, sort out the van and have a well earned coffee and sandwich. Later, we take Kelly for a walk and let him graze.

7pm: Go down into Hexham for a meal with a couple of friends. Afterwards, we return to the race-course, final feed and rug up for Kelly, and walk down to the camping area where we have a jolly get-together – the only time a lot of us meet up is at rides.

· THURSDAY 23rd ·

7am: Feed Kelly and return to the tent for breakfast. Then I go for a ride, and Wendy goes down into Hexham to shop.

12.30pm: Wendy arrives back and we have lunch, going over the race route and the best places to meet up. I usually only have one crew but a friend, Paul Saville, has offered to drive up from London and help. He isn't expected to arrive until the next day. In the afternoon we leave the race-course and drive around from one checkpoint to another working out the riding time against the driving time, allowing a little extra for Saturday traffic.

5pm: Arrive back at the stables and while Wendy makes a much needed cup of coffee I collect Kelly so he can stretch his legs and graze. Later, we settle him for the night – Wendy fills the water containers ready for Saturday as the water pressure is very low and it takes ages to fill an ordinary bucket.

8pm: Go down into Hexham for a meal. We have discovered a very good hotel where the owner is a keen huntsman. We return to check and feed Kelly, then make our way to the big tent for another get-together.

· FRIDAY 24th ·

7.30am: Groom and lunge Kelly for about 45 minutes; then he is allowed to graze. Wendy starts going through all the equipment for the next day. The weather is very hot so we will need a great deal of water for washing down as well as drinking. Wendy and I need one or two things from Hexham so we race down to the shops before they get

Jill Thomas and Egyptian Khalifa on the Three Rivers Ride, 1987 (John Watts Photography)

too busy. Kelly doesn't kick, but the ride has a massed start and there is always somebody who will use your horse's rear-end as a buffer; so I am going to tie a red ribbon to his tail. I would sooner people thought he kicked than have a horse with cut up back legs (or worse).

10am: I clean my tack and Wendy gets my weights sorted out, and makes up my Isostar drink. This is far better than anything else I have tried when racing. It tastes pretty awful until your body needs it, and then it tastes like nectar. This is carried in a 'bum bag' around my waist and at each checkpoint all I have to do is hand my crew the empty bottle, and they hand me a full one.

Paul arrives and after a quick bite to eat and a drink he and Wendy go out onto the course for the rest of the morning. This gives me a chance to stick my bikini top on and enjoy the sun, combining sunbathing with tack cleaning. My saddle was placed in the van ready for later that afternoon when I would have to weigh in.

1pm: Seeing as my crew is still absent and the heat is still tempting, I take the route description and my map outside and spend a rather lazy hour studying. Then Paul and Wendy return and make detailed lists of who goes where and when.

2.30pm: After feeding Kelly the three of us make our way to the briefing. This is held on the grass outside the bar and is quite a light-hearted affair to start with. We are talked through various parts of the route and told that if two horses cross the finish line together they will not share a place but will be separated into 1st, 2nd, etc. The vets also give a talk about possible heat problems, and stress that we must be careful and make sure the horses are given every chance to drink.

After the briefing we fetch Kelly for the vetting.

4pm: We are among the first and it is a funny feeling to be in the main parade ring – especially as my horse is so laid back and blasé about it all. His lumps and bumps are inspected, his heart rate is taken and then in front of all the vets he is trotted the full length of the ring and back so they all have the chance to note any odd action. Kelly plaits his hind legs. He only does it when he is being led and it does annoy me.

4.30pm: I want to work Kelly on the lunge again; my crew load the water containers and fill the extra ones that Paul has brought with him. Several people watch me work Kelly, and a very nice lady enquired if I was riding, and in which class. Very proudly I inform her Class One. 'Oh, really!' was the amazed response. It is not my fault that my horse refuses to waste any energy at all, and is so narrow that front end on he resembles a clothes peg. I could give him a month's rest on full rations and still not get a firework display from him.

5.30pm: Feed Kelly; make up the evening and early morning feeds – all they need is damping down. His meals are made up of pony cubes, oats, sugar beet, a vitamin supplement, cod liver oil and carrots. After a ride he has a small amount of bran as well.

6.30pm: Dressed in all my riding clothes we drive up to the weighing room. Panic! It seems that I am 7lb (3kg) light. After much rushing around Val Long lends me two sheets each weighing $3\frac{1}{2}$lb ($1\frac{1}{2}$kg) (I am already carrying 8lb (3.6kg) around my waist). We decide to eat first, and then Paul will fix the lead into my saddle.

9.15pm: I take my time rugging and feeding Kelly, thinking over how I intend to ride. This is not something that can be done beforehand as there is the weather to be taken into account, plus the going, how often you can see your crew and so on. As Wendy has a final run-through of the gear, Paul fixes the lead. It is then decided to try it on and amid much hilarity I am put aboard, no stirrups and just a head collar. Paul leads me around the yard at a trot, not very nice as the yard is on the side of a steep hill! This done, Kelly is returned to his stable and rugged up again.

10.30pm: My crew send me to bed.

12.15am: It's no good – I am wide awake and raring to go, so I get up and feed Kelly. Although I return to bed it really is a waste of time as I am so wound up.

· SATURDAY 25th ·

1.15am: Wendy gives up and goes for a shower. We have a cup of coffee.

2am: I get up and go and groom Kelly. He really cannot understand what I am doing messing about in the middle of the night.

2.45am: Time to tack up and get out for a walk. Paul joins us and Wendy tells me where they will be – this way we will always have a good supply of water where it is needed. After the 25 mile gate Wendy will travel with Paul in the car, taking the van home when I am on the final leg of the ride. Paul would then stay on the course to see me in. Great arrangement and it worked well.

3am: Trot up. This is done by the light of car headlights, luckily very few horses were bothered by them. We spend the rest of the time walking around. I have tied a sponge to the front of my saddle with a long piece of string so when we cross water I can wash him off without actually getting off.

3.30am: We're off! Twenty-seven horses following a slow-moving car along the first three miles of road. To start we remain more or less together. I have my times worked out for 8–7–6mph, and aim to go for 8mph dropping no slower than 7mph.

When we leave the road I drop back to allow the front runners space. This gives me the chance to get into an easy rhythm much quicker than if the leaders were pulling us along.

Yvonne Tyson on Caligular (we rode most of the Golden Horseshoe together and got Bronze) caught up with me and we decided to stay together for a while. Although the morning was cool we were obviously in for a hot day. Scenery was spectacular in places and maintaining a good pace, it wasn't long before we were running into various back-up crews. When I saw Paul it was just to say we were going Okay.

The ride was uneventful up to the 25 mile gate. The route was very well marked and both Yvonne and I passed straight through the vetting into the first hold. I am in trouble for not drinking enough – as the day warms up I will make up for that.

From 25 to 50 miles the going is quite tough, and some of the tracks are very hard and stony – it only takes one misplaced foot and you end up with a bruised sole. Each time we meet our crew they wash Kelly thoroughly, handing me a gallon container of water that is poured over his neck. However, he is never touched before he has had the chance to drink and only when he has finished does the washing start.

· 50-MILE GATE ·

As soon as we cross into the gate area a vet takes the pulse. They do not tell me what it is, so you have to do your own and present to the vet as soon as it is below 64. On every check Kelly was in the 40s or very low 50s but I had to keep getting my crew to re-check. When you presented the horse to the vet, if the heart rate was low enough they did the one minute test to make sure that the horse was sound as well. During the hold Kelly is washed down, his saddle removed and he is offered a small feed. As this is the longest break of the day I have something to eat and drink.

Yvonne and I at this stage are in 11th and 12th place. Wendy helps me to replace the saddle, and very soon we are on our way again. The going is hard and stony and the forest tracks were by far the worst – at least on the moor it was softer. We start to overtake some of the riders ahead of us; both horses are working well with an easy pace.

As we start the last five miles to the 75 mile vet gate it is very hot and the weights around my waist have started to rub. We are still overtaking riders and yet have not quickened the pace at all. When we go into the 75 mile gate we are in 7th and 8th place.

· 75-MILE GATE ·

Wendy checks Kelly's pulse and it is so low we go straight to the vets, again it is checked and he has the one minute test. The saddle area is looked at for rubs, and when the vets are satisfied we are sent into the hold area.

I had to start slightly ahead of Yvonne and within a mile I had caught up with two other horses, staying with them for a short time due to the really rough track and also because I seemed suddenly to have run out of steam. It was then that I took to drinking as much Isostar as I could. Very soon my second wind arrived and off we sent again by ourselves. Kelly has a habit of spooking and slamming the brakes on; he did this quite out of the blue and then leapt forwards, jarring my neck badly (I had been told to ride with a support around my neck as I had at the Golden Horseshoe, following a car accident, but I had forgotten to pack it and was now paying the penalty).

By the time we arrived at the 90 mile gate I wasn't sure which was worse, my waist or my neck. Again we went straight through the vet gate into a five minute hold and Paul and Wendy went to work on Kelly, washing him off; they had decided the rider was either past help or tough enough to cope. Paul had to give me a leg-up (as he had all the way around) and we were on our way.

Within ten minutes, however, I had to get off to open a number of gates. I wasted time here and very soon Yvonne is back with me. As we pass our crews we are told that the rider in third place is just two minutes ahead, so with the pace hotting up it does not take long to catch her. One look at us bearing down and she takes off at a smart trot, but we stay in hot pursuit and as we round a corner we see the two leading horses.

We had not gone much further when Yvonne's horse caught his foot and they both went crashing down on the road.

I jumped off to help. Luckily although the road had been newly gravelled they had escaped serious injury. Yvonne soon remounted but as she felt faint we took it slowly down the wood track. This was a very steep downhill stony track with a stream at the bottom. Yvonne got off and washed Caligular down. I continue up the steep climb. When we had nearly got to the top Kelly caught his foot under a stone and fell. Fortune is smiling on us and he has just taken a little hair from his knee. Yvonne is in sight and we join forces to walk in the final half mile or so. It would have been a different story if we both had not fallen and a good racing finish would have had an interesting edge, especially a racing finish between five horses! We crossed the line with me in 4th place and Yvonne in 5th, subject of course to the vetting.

· 30 MINUTES TO VET ·

This is the make or break time: all the washing down is done with my crew's usual gusto and this time we get a little help from a friend (Val Long's crew Bev) – it is all a blur of frantic activity. I still have to weigh in and so cannot remove the blasted weight from my waist.

· VETTING ·

The pulse is checked and is fine, then he is trotted out and that is fine. All I can think is that my horse is fantastic, my crew are the best but that the rider needs improving.

· AFTERWARDS ·

Wendy takes Kelly, who is rugged up, to graze; he is tired but relaxed. A very nice young man takes my saddle to the weight room and I plonk myself unceremoniously on the scales. Here I find that during 13 hours of racing I have not lost any weight – credit must go to Paul and Wendy who kept a first-class eye on me and made me have food regardless of my 'I don't fancy anything'.

Paul leaves straightaway for London. Kelly is left in peace, and we have a meal. All evening we take it in turns to give him very small feeds and check that he hasn't broken out in a sweat. Wendy tries to phone through to Goodwood to find out how her mare Sahara Fiesta (John Brooker up) is getting on. Eventually she gets the news that her mare is going well and in the running.

10.30pm: I can no longer keep my eyes open and having nearly fallen asleep on my feet in the bar, I decide to have a final look at Kelly and bed.

. SUNDAY 26TH ·

6am: Feed and check Kelly; Wendy is still in bed. When she surfaces we have a cup of coffee, then I take Kelly out to graze and walk. He is not in the least stiff, and considering what he had done the day before is in good condition. Pop Kelly back in his stable and we have a wander around. The rain and mist which came during Saturday evening puts a real damper on the event.

9.30am: Slowly make our way to the parade ring for the international vetting. People start gathering to watch as the vets begin to take heart rates, and one at a time we have to trot right around the ring. The drizzle stops and the sun starts to show. We are then asked to return (with our horses) for the prize-giving.

10.30am: We all start to mingle in a rather large group and one at a time are called up to receive our prizes. The bottle that I won was given to Wendy straightaway and my thanks with it. It is a light-hearted affair and many new friends were made.

By mid-morning Kelly is back in his stable, some riders and crews are leaving; Wendy and I go through all the gear, loading the van to make it easy to find things during the return journey.

4pm: I bring Kelly down by the tent to graze which gives me the chance to chat to other owners doing the same thing. The bad weather had cleared away and it was a thoroughly pleasant interlude.

8pm: Several people who were staying overnight decided to go into Hexham for a good meal. Thus I ended up driving a van-load of people off the race-course. The meal was eaten in the usual high spirits, helped along by the fact that Wendy had phoned Goodwood and been told her mare had won 4th place. This led to double celebrations, great for all but the driver (me). Needless to say once home and when the horses had been checked and fed I joined in the celebrations until the early hours.

Monday and Tuesday will be long hours travelling, with an overnight stop with Liz Finney again. Kelly will be unloaded more to allow for the fact that he will be more tired. David is due to meet us at Exeter Services, and while Wendy drives to Dorset, he will take over and drive us to the bottom of Cornwall.

It was a great event from the start to the finish, the people were friendly, and the ride well organised. I would do it again even though the next one will not be exactly the same.

The training for the ride was no different from Kelly's usual routine. Monday to Friday I lunge him for 30 minutes before I go to work. Then anything from 8 to 16 miles are ridden in the afternoon. He gets either Saturday or Sunday off and the one he works can be a ride of up to 20 miles. Of course, he has to go to local shows, not because he's any good, but we are a minor celebrity pair in the area, and it's good to be seen – if it promotes the sport I'd go every day of the week.

Kelly will be rested for five days, then for a week he will work quietly doing about 10 miles a day, going back into training on the second week. His next 100 mile ride will be in September and he has two 40 mile rides to do in between. Of course, if he doesn't feel or look well then it will be played very much by ear – where horses are concerned, nothing is cut and dried.

PEN PORTRAITS
· *JOAN ALLEN* ·

Joan Allen (14.10.18) from Hertfordshire came to long distance riding after a varied competitive career with horses which included competing at Badminton Three Day Event. She has competed in point-to-points, Arab racing, horse trials, dressage, show-jumping driving and has shown hacks and hunters, all to a high level.

Joan has a farming background and is a qualified riding instructor – she has been chief instructor at her local Pony Club for many years. She has won numerous medals in major (set speed) rides in Great Britain. She won the Goodwood International once, taken second position once, and had numerous placings. On her first attempt in the National Championships (Three Rivers Ride) she was placed second.

Her numerous successes abroad include riding in the 1984 Vienna–Budapest Ride in which she finished in 9th place. In the following year she took part in the Brittany ride (Raid d'endurance Du Tregor), finished second and took the 'best foreign rider' title. She has also represented Britain in the North American Open Endurance Championships.

She helped the British team to victory in Belgium, and took second place individually, and took individual 11th place in the 1987 European Championships in Erlangen, Germany.

Joan's horse, Pondicherry, is a chestnut, 14.2hh Anglo Arab mare out of Country Sunshine by Samson (born in 1976).

Joan Allen and Pondicherry encounter one of the many gates on Exmoor (Bob Langrish)

· *DAVID ABERCOMBIE* ·

David Abercombie (6.8.44) is a self-employed plumbing and heating engineer by trade and took up riding for the first time in 1977 as a release from work. He took up long distance riding seriously in 1983.

1987 was a particularly good year for David and his horse Balou – he won the 'distance rider' national championship for top rider, and the horse won the same trophy for top horse.

Two years before the Cambridgeshire-based team had won gold both on the Golden Horseshoe ride (100 miles – 160km), and on the Peak District Open in Derbyshire. In 1986 they competed in their first 100 mile ride at Cheltenham, and were fourth in the National Championship (Three Rivers Ride).

Their most successful year, 1987, began with a placing of sixth position on the Summer Solstice (100 mile – 160km) in Nottinghamshire. The following month they achieved gold in the Black Mountains Ride in Wales (110 miles – 176.9km). Then in September they were runners-up in the 1987 National Championship ride.

David's horse, Balou, is a blue roan 16hh seven-eighths Thoroughbred gelding by the HIS premium stallion Brioche out of Bellams White Heather (born in 1976).

· *CHARLOTTE BEARD* ·

Charlotte Beard (28.3.68) made a name for herself as a top junior rider. She started riding when she was seven; her mother, Ann, had always ridden and took up long distance riding when Charlotte was ten. She followed suit at the age of twelve, and quickly achieved success.

She won the EHPS Junior Championship two years running in 1981 and 1982 riding a 13hh Arab/Welsh pony Bychan Melody. In 1982 she was joint second in the Red Dragon 50 mile (80km) endurance race in Wales and won the Peter Ball Trophy for the most points over 40 miles. The following year she was reserve Junior Champion on a 14.2hh Arab mare Romanina.

1985 was a particularly successful one for Charlotte. With her 14.2hh Arab mare Cariad she won the New Forest 50 mile endurance ride, and the Breamore 50 mile endurance ride, setting a new record of 14.02mph on the latter.

In 1987 she began competing with Maniquin, jointly owned by herself and her mother, and they were sixth in the National Championships (Three Rivers Ride). Maniquin is a 15.2hh chestnut Anglo Arab mare by Val Long's Tarim out of Crimson Flame (born in 1980).

· CATHY BROWN ·

Cathy Brown is an English rider who has been based in France since 1973, and is a former nurse and midwife. She runs a small stud producing pure and part Egyptian Arab horses for showing, racing and endurance riding.

Most of her achievements have been in France and Cathy has done particularly well in the ELDRIC Trophy. In 1984 she was the French Lightweight Endurance Champion and the following year took the vice-champion title. In the same year she was fifth in the ELDRIC Trophy. In 1986 she took part in the World Championships in Rome with Zoltan, her top horse through 1984, 1985 and 1986.

With her second horse Naquib she has had four victories in major rides in Great Britain and France. Firstly he won the 300km (186 miles) three day ride Chevauchée du Gers, and 12 days later came third in the French 138km (120 miles) Allan ride. Then they went on to win Breamore in June, the French Florac in September (equal first) and the Goodwood 100 mile ride in October. In 1987 she took the title of vice-champion in the ELDRIC Trophy.

Naquib is a grey 15.2hh Arab stallion by Dahman out of Jamila (born in 1979), Zoltan was a grey 15.3hh part Arab gelding by Ann Hyland's Nizzolan out of Magnet Regent (a trotting mare who had competed in 100 milers in America).

· LARISSA CAMPBELL ·

Larissa Campbell (25.7.67) learned to ride at the age of five; she was a keen Pony Club member, and hunted before taking up long distance riding.

With her horse Sundance Boy she won the silver medal in the Golden Horseshoe Ride on Exmoor in 1987. A month later she was third in the Avon Valley 60 mile (96km) ride. The Warwickshire-based student then went on to become the 1987 National Champion on the Three Rivers Ride.

Sundance Boy was unable to compete in the 1988 Golden Horseshoe Ride, but borrowing Valerie Cooper's Witham Golden Colonel, Larissa won a bronze medal.

A palomino, Sundance Boy is a 15hh gelding (born in 1978).

· CANDY CAMERON ·

Candy Cameron (14.2.53) is Scotland's top rider. She runs a riding school in Inverness-shire and is a founder member of the Highland Long Distance Riding Club.

She has won the Scottish Championship three times in a row – 1986,

Liz Finney and Showgirl II cross the finish at Exford (Bob Langrish)

1987 and 1988 – on three different horses. In 1987 she also won the Scottish mini-marathon with White Trooper, and with the same horse took fifth position in the Arab Horse Society Marathon.

On the 1988 Golden Horseshoe ride she received a 100 mile completion rosette.

White Trooper is a 15.1hh grey part Arab gelding, born in 1979, and out of Bunty Macby White Falcon.

· *LIZ FINNEY* ·

Liz Finney (21.6.45) has had a lot of success with Cath Kennedy's horse Showgirl II. She lives in Cheshire and is a pharmacist.

Riding another of Cath Kennedy's horses, Cleo, Liz took a Silver award on the Golden Horseshoe Ride and took a Gold award on the Black Mountains Ride.

With Showgirl II in 1984 she was in the silver medal winning team at Florac in France, and achieved 5th place at the Goodwood International ride with Cleo.

In 1985 she and Showgirl II won the National Championships at Salisbury, were sixth in the Goodwood International Ride, and took part in the European Championships in Austria.

They became National Champions in 1986, took sixth place in the Goodwood International and were reserves for the World Championships. Liz and Showgirl II won a gold medal on the Golden Horseshoe ride then went on to win individual silver at the European Championships in Germany. The team, of which they were members, took fourth place.

In 1988 they won the only silver award on the Golden Horseshoe and Liz was awarded the title of Top Lady and the Maxwell Perpetual Award from the National Light Horse Breeding Society.

Showgirl II is a brown 16hh mare by HIS stallion Quadriga (born in 1976).

· *PAM JAMES* ·

Pam James (2.6.48) has been a key member of a number of British teams and has had a lot of success with her horses Saxon and Forest Fox. She is based in Gwent and works full-time as a secretary.

With Saxon, her first long distance horse, she won four Golden Horseshoe gold medals and two international team gold medals. Sadly, he had to be put down after a tragic road accident in 1981.

From 1981 riding Forest Fox she achieved three Golden Horseshoe gold medals and a silver in the first 100 mile Golden Horseshoe ride in 1986.

Leaving Forest Fox behind, Pam went to America to compete with a

Val Long and Arab stallion Tarim, three times winners of the Summer Solstice
(Bob Langrish)

borrowed horse in the Tevis Cup ride, and is one of three British riders to hold a Tevis Buckle.

1986 saw the combination helping the British team to the gold medal in the World Championships in Rome; they were sixth individually. In the same year they were fifth at Goodwood International.

In the following year they were members of the British team in the European Championships but a cut pastern meant that they were eliminated.

They were among 65 competitors on the Mousquetaire Ride from Windsor to Paris in 1987. Pam and Forest Fox were in the Mouton Cadet sponsored team which finished second, and were individually 6th.

Forest Fox is a bay 15.3hh three-quarter Thoroughbred mare by Blandford Lad (born in 1977).

· *VAL LONG* ·

Val Long (26.1.48) has had a lot of success with her Arab stallion Tarim, at home and abroad. She began long distance riding in 1973 on a New Forest pony and they won the first competition they entered – a 40 mile ride. After that she was hooked.

Val bought Tarim as a six-month-old colt soon after this. He was broken in as a four-year-old and won a 25 mile ride in the autumn of the same year.

In 1984 in an exciting racing finish they won the Summer Solstice in Nottinghamshire and set a new British record for 100 miles (160km), of nine hours and forty-nine minutes. The following day he was awarded the best condition trophy. In the same year they were second at Breamore.

Two years later, 1986, Val and Tarim again won the Summer Solstice in Nottinghamshire and were third at Breamore. They were fourth individually in the World Championships in Rome and took second place in the ELDRIC Trophy. Riding Legend Alcoran, Val also took third place at Goodwood that year.

In 1987 they achieved seventh place in the European Championships in Erlangen and was equal tenth at Breamore.

In 1988 they once again won the Summer Solstice, this time at Hexham, and were selected to ride in the World Championships in America.

Val, who lives in Dyfed, is sponsored by Endurance Clothing and Badminton Horse Feeds. She has won the Martini Horse Award for Endurance three years running, in 1985, 1986 and 1987.

Tarim is a dark chestnut 15.2hh Arab stallion by Luachim (born in 1976).

· *KAY TRIGG* ·

Kay Trigg (28.7.52) of Staffordshire has had many achievements with her horse Brookhouse Maestro. In 1985 they won a silver award in the Black Mountains 110 mile (176km) ride, and in the following year took seventh place in the National Championships.

Her horse won the best part-bred Arab trophy on the Golden Horseshoe ride in 1987 in which they won another silver award. A month later they took fourth place and the best 14.2hh or under trophy in the Open British Championships (EHPS). In the following September they were third in the National Championships then went on to take part in the Mousquetaire Windsor to Paris Ride. The team took second place, they were sixth individually and Brookhouse Maestro was presented with the best condition award.

They finished 1987 in second place on the BHS points table, with fourth place in the 'Distance Rider' championship, and a member of the number one team.

Brookhouse Maestro is a chestnut 14.1hh part-bred Arab gelding by Muston Sol (born in 1977).

· MARGARET WILKES ·

Margaret Wilkes (6.5.48) has had much success with Wyere Lad – she bought this horse as a foal from Llanybyther Horse Mart, sold him, then bought him back again! As a four-year-old in 1979 he won his first competition, a 25 mile novice ride at the Red Dragon in Wales. A year later he won the Red Dragon's 50 mile open endurance ride, beating the European champion Judy Beaumont in a racing finish.

In 1982 they won the 50 mile open at Breamore. Four years later they won the two-day 100 mile Red Dragon Ride.

1987 was a remarkable year for Margaret and Wyere Lad. They won the 50 mile open endurance ride at Lincoln, breaking Charlotte Beard's record time with 14.77mph. A month later they completed the Summer Solstice – in spite of getting lost for over an hour, Wyere Lad raced in and finished in second place, only to be eliminated because he was slightly lame.

In the following month they won the Red Dragon ride, and in September they won the New Forest 60 mile endurance ride. They then took part in the Arab Horse Society Marathon in October at Belvoir Castle, finished 4th, and won the best part-bred Arab trophy.

In 1988 they achieved 100 mile completion in the Golden Horseshoe Ride and won the Goodwood International Ride in 12hr 30min. They were selected to represent Britain in the World Championships.

Wyere Lad is a grey 15.1hh part-bred Arab gelding by Sollum (AHSB) out of a cob/Thoroughbred, cross mare (born in 1974).

APPENDICES

1: RIDE RESULTS

Red Dragon

1979 (50 miles – 80km)

Placing/ Speed	Rider	Horse	Breed	Height	Sex	Age
1/7.075	J. Ware	Cairo	Arab	15hh	S	11
2/7.075	S. Humphreys	Nizar	PB Arab	15.3hh	G	5
3/7.075	E. Langley	Philie	Thoroughbred	15.1hh	M	9
4/6.85	M. Montgomerie	Tarquin	U. Reg	15.1hh	G	16
5/6.14	T. Allen	Louchi	U.Reg	14.3hh	G	6
6/6.06	D. Francis	Harvey	U. Reg	–	G	–

1980 (50 Miles – 80km)

1/8.159	M. Wilkes	Wyere Lad	PB Arab	15.1hh	G	6
2/8.159	J. Beaumont	Fforest Orchid	Appaloosa	15.1hh	M	9
3/8.152	C. Greasley	Roxena	Arab	–	M	9
4/7.81	M. Montgomerie	Tarquin	U. Reg	15.1hh	G	17
5/7.54	D. Francis	Boston Bay	Thoroughbred	15.3hh	G	7
6/7.15	V. Haywood	Dresden	U. Reg	14.2hh	G	10

1981 (75 miles – 120km)

1/6.7	V. Haywood	Dresden	U. Reg	14.2hh	G	11

1982 (50 miles – 80km)
DAY ONE

1	V. Long	Tarim	Arab	15.2hh	S	6
2	D. Toomer-Baker	Nimrodel	Anglo/Trak	16hh	M	8
=3	D. Whitehead	Sundown Poppy	U. Reg	14hh	M	9
=3	L. Whitehead	Arabella	U. Reg	15.1hh	M	10
=3	D. Francis	Copper Knob II	U. Reg	16hh	G	–
=3	T. Graham	Pitvale Golden Boy	PB Arab	15.1hh	G	10
7	B. Brigg	Reproach	Thoroughbred	15.1hh	G	10

DAY TWO (50 miles – 80km)

1/8	V. Haywood	Dresden	U. Reg	14.2hh	G	12
2/7.87	D. Toomer-Baker	Nimrodel	Anglo/Trak	16hh	M	8
3/6.68	D. Francis	Copper Knob II	U. Reg	16hh	G	–
4/6.69	D. Whitehead	Sundown Poppy	U. Reg	14hh	M	9
5/6.66	W. Longbottom	Shawon Dasee	Arab	15.2hh	S	10
6/6.04	B. Brigg	Reproach	Thoroughbred	15.1hh	G	10
Jun/7.81	C. Beard	Bychan Melody	PB Arab/Welsh	13.1hh	M	8

1983 (100 miles [160km] over two days)
DAY ONE

1/7.62	D. Francis	Boston Bay	Thoroughbred	15.3hh	G	9
2/7.62	D. Toomer-Baker	Nimrodel	Anglo/Trak	16hh	M	9
3/7.56	V. Haywood	Dresden	U. Reg	14.2hh	G	13
4/7.49	A. Beard	Wahid	Arab	15hh	G	8
5/7.18	L. Whitehead	Arabella	U. Reg	15.1hh	M	11
6/7.17	D. Whitehead	Sundown Poppy	U. Reg	14hh	M	10

DAY TWO

1/7.84	V. Haywood	Dresden	U. Reg	16hh	G	13
2/7.83	D. Toomer-Baker	Nimrodel	Anglo/Trak	16hh	M	9
3/7.65	H. Maurer	Chaber	PB Arab	15.2hh	G	7
4/5.81	D. Whitehead	Sundown Poppy	U. Reg	14hh	M	10
5/5.80	L. Whitehead	Arabella	U. Reg	15.1hh	M	11
6/5.51	D. Holloway	Lugie	U. Reg	13.3hh	M	9
7/5.50	W. Longbottom	Shawon Dasee	Arab	15.2hh	S	11

1984 (100 miles – 160km over two days)
DAY ONE
All horses were eliminated as all ran out of time

DAY TWO

1/7.12	C. Hull	William	U. Reg	15.1hh	G	9
2/7.11	C. Beard	Cariad	Arab	14.2hh	M	7
3/7.10	S. Scorey	Squire Tebeldi	U. Reg	14.3hh	G	10

1985 (100 miles (160km) over two days)
DAY ONE
All horses were eliminated as all ran out of time

DAY TWO
All horses were eliminated as all ran out of time

1986 (100 miles [160km] over two days)
DAY ONE

1/7.69	P. Amies	Rufus	U.Reg	15.1hh	G	9
2/7.69	Y. Tyson	Caligular	Arab	15.1hh	G	7
3/7.61	L. Dunn	Bonanza	Arab	15hh	S	10
4/7.15	G. Hellman	Bucklesham Camila	Welsh C	13hh	M	10

DAY TWO
No placings, only completions

1987 (100 miles [160km] over two days)

1	M. Wilkes	Wyere Lad	PB Arab	15.1hh	G	13
2	C. Hull	Daisy	PB Arab	14.2hh	M	10

Breamore

1978 (50 miles – 80km)

1	J. Nicholson	Granby Louisa	Anglo Arab	15.2hh	M	7
=2	M. Montgomerie	Brig O'Doon	P.B. Arab	15.3hh	G	8
=2	A. Hyland	Nizzolan	Arab	15.1hh	S	11

4	L. Oliver	Shaaban	Arab	15.2hh	G	5
Junior	J. Ware	Cairo	Arab	15hh	S	10

1979 (54 miles – 86km)

1	L. Oliver	Shaaban	Arab	15.2hh	G	6
2	J. Ware	Cairo	Arab	15hh	S	11
3	A. Ware	Kazmahal	Arab	15.1hh	G	7
4	M. Montgomerie	Tarquin	U. Reg	15.1hh	G	16
5	J. Davies	Nossan Lad	Arab	14.3hh	G	8
6	E. Hoole	Badger		15hh	G	10

1980 (54 miles – 86km)

1/9.5	F. Waycott	Farona	Arab	14.3hh	M	7
2/9.5	S. Humphreys	Nizar	PB Arab	15.3hh	G	8
3/8.97	M. Montgomerie	Tarquin	U. Reg	15.1hh	G	17
4/8.97	L. Beaney	Magnus	Arab	14hh	S	10

1981 (52 miles – 83km)

1/13.0	C. Grant	Magic Sun	Arab	14.2hh	S	9
2/12.79	J. Beaumont	Fforest Orchid	Appaloosa	15.1hh	M	10
3/11.91	P. Maxwell	Leewood Isolde	PB Arab	15.1hh	M	7
4/1.22	A. Ware	Shaaban	Arab	15.3hh	G	8
5/10.61	F. Waycott	Farona	Arab	14.3hh	M	8
6/10.23	D. Toomer-Baker	Nimrodel	Anglo/Trak	16hh	M	6

1982 (50 miles – 80km)

1/14	B. Newby	Wyere Lad	PB Arab	15.1hh	G	8
2/14	V. Long	Tarim	Arab	15.2hh	S	6
3/13.8	J. Allen	Inca	U. Reg	15.1hh	M	9
=4/13.5	P. Mobsby	Caradoc March Past	U. Reg	15hh	G	15
=4/13.5	D. Toomer-Baker	Nimrodel	Anglo/Trak	16hh	M	8
6/12.6	M. Montgomerie	Tarquin	U. Reg	15.1hh	G	19

1983 (50 miles – 80km)

1/12.0	H. Maurer	Chaba	PB Arab	15.2hh	G	7
2/11.2	D. Toomer-Baker	Nimrodel	Anglo/Trak	16hh	M	9
3/10.3	B. Vaughan	Tudor Legend	U. Reg	15.1hh	G	8
4/10.3	V. Haywood	Dresden	U. Reg	14.2hh	G	13
5/9.8	M. Butler	My Crispin	U. Reg	15.1hh	G	9

1984 (50 miles – 80km)

1/12.14	V. Cooper	Witham Golden Colonel	U. Reg	15.1hh	G	11
2/12.14	V. Long	Tarim	Arab	15.2hh	S	8
3/11.71	M. Whiteley	Caswell Easter Surprise	PB Arab	15.2hh	G	10
4/11.45	D. Toomer-Baker	Nimrodel	Anglo/Trak	16hh	M	10
=5/11.27	A. Ware	Shaaban	Arab	15.3hh	G	11
=5/11.27	D. Boots	Hollington Dancing Flame	PB Arab	14.2hh	M	14

1985 (50 miles – 80km)

1/14.03	C. Beard	Cariad	Arab	14.2hh	M	7
2/13.8	C. Tuggey	El Askar	Arab	14.3hh	G	10
3/12.71	P. James	Forest Fox	³/₄ Thoroughbred	15.3hh	M	9
4/12.70	J. Reeve	Siouxtika Rey	PB Arab	15.3hh	M	10
5/11.11	M Barrett	Baccarat	TB/Haflinger	14.2hh	M	14
6/10.60	H. Blair	Solfried	Haflinger	13.3hh	G	10

1986 (50 miles – 80km)

1/12.7	L. Dunn	Bonanza	Arab	15hh	S	10
2/12.6	D. Toomer-Baker	Nimrodel	Anglo/Trak	16hh	M	12
3/12.3	V. Long	Tarim	Arab	15.2hh	S	10
4/11.6	C. Acquer	Persian Swallow	Arab	15hh	M	8
5/11.1	C. Brown	Zoltan	PB Arab	16hh	G	13
6/11.1	J. Brooker	Lady Amblya	PB Arab	14.2hh	M	9

1987 (50 miles – 80km)

1/12.6	C. Brown	Naquib	Arab	15hh	S	8
2/12.6	J. Brooker	Lady Amblya	PB Arab	14.2hh	M	10
3/12.5	D. Francis	Evesbatch Excalibur	U. Reg	16hh	G	8
4/11.9	V. Cooper	Legend Alcoran	PB Arab	15hh	G	8
5/11.5	M. Drummond	Rosy	Thoroughbred	15.2hh	M	9
6/11.4	M. Barrett	Baccarat	TB/Haflinger	14.2hh	M	16

1988 (50 miles – 80km)

1/11.14	S. Nash	Gemini	U. Reg	15.1hh	G	9
2/11.4	D. Passant	Feranoush	Arab	15.2hh	M	14
3/11	J. Allen	Pondicherry	Anglo/Arab	14.2hh	M	13
4/10.6	P. Mobsby	Kings Shakira	PB Arab	15.2hh	M	9
5/10.3	Y. Tyson	Crystal Calif	Arab	15.2hh	G	9
6/10.2	S. Vaughan	Zimir	Arab	15hh	G	13

Summer Solstice

1980 (100 miles [160km] in one day) Plumpton

1/7.246	J. Beaumont	Fforest Orchid	Appaloosa	15.1hh	M	9
=2/6.098	C. Greasley	Roxena	Arab	–	M	8
=2/8.098	M. Montgomerie	Tarquin	U. Reg	15.1hh	G	17
4/6.05	V. Haywood	Dresden	U. Reg	14.2hh	G	10

1982 (100 miles [160km] in one day) Plumpton

1/7.43	D. Toomer-Baker	Nimrodel	Anglo/Trak	16hh	M	8
2/7.18	L. Harrison	Showgirl II	U. Reg	16hh	M	6
3/6.57	V. Haywood	Dresden	U. Reg	14.2hh	G	12
=4/6.45	P. Guerin	Cleo	U. Reg	15.2hh	M	9
=4/6.45	I. Hasbad	Florett	Connemara/Fjord	14.2hh	G	12
=4/6.45	L. Wall	Rowen Ceri	Welsh Cob	14hh	M	15
7/4.89	W. Longbottom	Shawon Dasee	Arab	15.2hh	S	10

1983 (100 miles [160km] in one day) Plympton

1/7.8	D. Toomer-Baker	Nimrodel	Anglo/Trak	16hh	M	9
2/7.2	V. Haywood	Dresden	U. Reg	14.2hh	G	13
3/7.0	P. Guerin	Cleo	U. Reg	15.2hh	M	10

4/7.0	G. Shutt	Triella	PB Arab	15.2hh	M	10
5/6.1	P. Holloway	Clementine	U. Reg	15hh	M	16
6/–	D. Whitehead	Sundown Poppy	U. Reg	14hh	M	10
7/–	W. Longbottom	Shawon Dasee	Arab	15.2hh	S	11

1984 (100 miles [160km] in one day) Southwell

1/8.46	V. Long	Tarim	Arab	15.2hh	S	8
2/8.45	D. Toomer-Baker	Nimrodel	Anglo/Trak	16hh	M	10
3/8.44	G. Shutt	Triella	PB Arab	15.2hh	M	11
4/8.43	D. Boots	Hollington Dancing Flame	PB Arab	14.2hh	M	14
5/6.62	C. Hull	William	Hunter	15.1hh	G	9
6/6.28	P. Holloway	Clementine	U. Reg	15hh	M	17
7/6.27	J. Welcher	Kandy Bullard	³/₄ Thoroughbred	16hh	M	12

1985 (100 miles [160km] in one day) Southwell

1/9.17	J. Welcher	Kandy Bullard	³/₄ Thoroughbred	16hh	M	13
2/8.53	D. Holloway	Clementine	U. Reg	15hh	M	18
3/8.52	J. Martin	Swansong of Shamala	Arab	15.2hh	G	16
4/6.59	E. Carradine	Solfried	Haflinger	13.3hh	G	10
5/6.58	H. Blair	Moondust	PB Arab	15hh	G	15
6/5.83	S. Scorey	Squire Tebeldi	U. Reg	14.2hh	G	11
7/5.82	V. Robinson	Pitfold Snowjel	Connemara/Arab	15hh	G	7

1986 (100 miles [160km] in one day) Southwell

1/9.57	V. Long	Tarim	Arab	15.2hh	S	10
2/9.56	J. Welcher	Kandy Bullard	³/₄ Thoroughbred	16hh	M	14
3/9.48	S. Scorey	Squire Tebeldi	U. Reg	14.2hh	G	12
4/8.89	L. Dunn	Bonanza	Arab	15hh	S	10
5/8.70	M. Butler	My Crispin	U. Reg	15.1hh	G	12
6/8.69	E. Martin	Sandpiper	U. Reg	12.1hh	G	12
7/8.68	J. Martin	Swansong of Shamala	Arab	15.2hh	G	17

1987 (100 miles [160km] in one day) Southwell

1/8.96	P. Amies	Rufus	U. Reg	15.1hh	G	10
2/8.81	J. McGuiness	Chadwyke Goodness Gracious Me	PB Arab	15.2hh	G	10
3/8.71	J. Timms	Jigsaw Puzzle	U. Reg	16hh	M	10
4/8.21	K. Trigg	Brookhouse Maestro	PB Arab	14.1hh	G	10
5/8.21	M. Barrett	Baccarat	TB/Haflinger	14.2hh	M	16
6/8.21	D. Abercombie	Balou	Thoroughbred	16hh	G	11

1988 (100 miles [160km] in one day) Hexham

1	V. Long	Tarim	Arab	15.2hh	S	12
2	C. Cameron	White Trooper	PB Arab	15.1hh	G	9
3	S. Nash	Gemini	U. Reg	15.1hh	G	9
4	J. Thomas	Egyptian	Arab	15.3hh	G	8
5	Y. Tyson	Caligular	Arab	15.1hh	G	8
6	J. Petherick	Lucinda	U. Reg	15.3hh	M	7
7	B. Wigley	Sushumi	–	15.1hh	M	16
8	P. Holloway	Silver Zora	Arab	14.2hh	M	13
9	J. Maddock	Sueh	PB Arab	15.3hh	G	11
10	P. King	Mr Magoo	PB Arab	15.2hh	G	9

Three Rivers/National Championships

1985 (80 miles – 128km gated ride)

1/6.98	J. Taylor	Beltane Phoenix	PB Arab	15hh	G	7
2/6.96	J. Jackson	Mulgrave Storm	–	16hh	M	10
3/6.95	M. Barrett	Baccarat	TB/Haflinger	14.2hh	M	14
4/–	J. Reeve	Siouxtika Rey	PB Arab	15hh	M	9
5/–	D. Abercombie	Balou	Thoroughbred	16hh	G	9
6/–	J. Allen	Pondicherry	Anglo/Arab	14.2hh	M	10

1986 (100 miles – 160km) First year of National Championships

1/8.54	L. Finney	Showgirl II	Thoroughbred	16hh	M	10
2/8.47	J. Allen	Pondicherry	Anglo/Arab	14.2hh	M	11
3/8.44	C. Brown	Shireen Lailee				
4/7.46	D. Abercombie	Balou	Thoroughbred	16hh	G	10
5/7.41	A. Uttley	Sheba	Arab	14.2hh	M	8
6/7.27	G. Webb	Londiani	Arab	15.1hh	G	7

1987 (100 miles – 160km)

1/7.59	L. Campbell	Sundance Boy	Palomino	14.2hh	G	9
2/7.26	D. Abercombie	Balou	Thoroughbred	16hh	G	10
3/7.22	K. Trigg	Brookhouse Maestro	Arab	14.2hh	G	10
4/–	D Passant	Ferhanoush	Arab	15.1hh	M	13
5/–	P. Cain	Ginger II	–	14.2hh	M	9
6/–	C. Beard	Maniquin	Anglo/Arab	15.2hh	M	7

1988 (100 miles [160km] in one day) Hexham

1/7.58	V. Long	Tarim	Arab	15.2hh	S	12
2/7.58	C. Cameron	White Trooper	PB Arab	15.1hh	G	9
3/7.58	S. Nash	Gemini	U. Reg	15.1hh	G	9
4/7.48	J. Thomas	Egyptian	Arab	15.3hh	G	8
5/7.48	Y. Tyson	Caligular	Arab	15.1hh	G	8
6/7.24	J. Petherick	Lucinda	U. Reg	15.3hh	M	7
7/7.11	B. Wigley	Sushumi	–	15.1hh	M	16
8/7.11	P. Holloway	Silver Zora	Arab	14.2hh	M	13
9/6.53	J. Maddock	Sueh	PB Arab	15.3hh	G	11
10/6.52	P. King	Mr Magoo	PB Arab	15.2hh	G	9

Golden Horseshoe

1979 (75 miles – 129km)

Award	Rider	Horse		*Height*	*Sex*	*Age*
Gold	Mrs M. Burton	Miss Muffet		14.2hh	M	9
Silver	Mrs L. Jackson	Setra		15hh	M	9
	Mrs C. Holloway	Oscar Wilde		15.2hh	G	6
Bronze	Mrs B. Hake	Homelands Major		14.2hh	G	9
	Miss S. Hatton	Jubilee Royale		15.2hh	M	6
	Mrs P. Parker	Spring Frolic		15.2hh	G	5
	Miss G. Barber	Mary Poppins		15.2hh	M	10
	Miss V. Barber	Popcorn		15.2hh	G	10
	Mrs M. Murray	Kestrel		15hh	M	9
	Mrs S. Robins	Winston II		15.2hh	G	8
	Mrs C. Breese	Ammon		15hh	S	6

1980 (75 miles – 129km)

Gold	Mrs J. Baker	Royal Caesar	15.3hh	G	6
	Mrs P. James	Saxon	15.3hh	G	12
	Mrs G. Shutt	Scylla	14.3hh	M	12
	Mrs M. Robinson	Maelor	15hh	M	11
	Mrs J. Beaumont	Fforest Orchid	15.1hh	M	10
	Mrs K. Bywater	Glanyrafon Rosita	15.2hh	M	9
Silver	Mrs L. Jackson	Setra	15hh	M	11
	Mrs J. Wrinch	Maestro	14.1hh	G	12
	Mrs M. Whiting	Moonfield Brandysnap	14.1hh	G	10
	Mrs M. Wall	St George	15hh	G	9
	Mrs F. Ogilvy	Poste Haste	15.1hh	M	6
Bronze	Mrs M. Eld	Beaver	16hh	G	14
	Mrs S. Hatton	Jubilee Royale	15.2hh	M	7
	Mrs C. Holloway	Cardoc	14hh	G	6
	Mrs F. Dixon	Zerena	15.1hh	M	9
	Mrs J. Martin	Coxwold Whisper	15.2hh	M	10
	Mrs J. Allen	Inca	15.1hh	M	8
	Mrs A. O'Brien	Smokey Joe	15.hh	G	13
	Mrs P. Piper	Honey Island	15hh	G	18

1981 (75 miles – 129km)

Gold	Mrs B. Johns	Benjamin
	Mrs J. Allen	Inca
	Mrs D. Davies	Zerrey
	Mrs A. Bartholomew	Lupin
	Mrs J. Baker	Royal Caesar
	Mrs S. Derby	Souessa
	Mrs P. James	Saxon
	Mrs K. Burrows	Honeyboy Zimba
	Miss S. Burrows	Vodka
	Mrs M. Butler	My Crispin
	Miss J. Devote	The Haggis
	Mrs E. French	Glasmyndd Honey
	Miss J. Powell	Autumn Enchantress
	Mr M. Sinclair	Copper Nob IV
	Mr D. Francis	Boston Bay
	Mrs V. Hayward	Dresden
	Miss S. Hatton	Jubilee Royale
	Mrs C. Kennedy	Treble Chance
	Mrs F. Fortune	Candlelight
	Mr D. Davey	Myne-Own
	Mrs M. Townley	Miss Muffet
	Mrs P. Piper	Honey Island
	Mrs F. Ogilvy	Poste Haste
	Mrs B. Dean	Jumbo Lad
	Mrs C. Sparks	Winston II
	Mrs L. Howell	Sovereign Spirit
	Mrs M. Whiting	Moonfield Brandysnap
	Mrs C. Hake	Crackerjack II
	Miss H. Blair	Moondust
	Mrs M. Morgan	Wimblestone Blue Dusk
	Mrs M. Miller	Fritz

	Miss A. Baggaley	Maxwell			
	Mrs K. Bywater	Glanyrafon Rosita			
	Mrs Copeley-Williams	Syllabub			
	Miss G. Barber	Mary Poppins			
	Miss V. Barber	Tarquin II			
	Mrs M. Windard	Canada Dry			
	Miss J. Shepherd	Crystal Czar			
	Mrs F. Dixon	Zerena			
	Mr B. Snell	Holford Honey			
	Mrs L. Jackson	Setra			
	Mrs A. Holland	J.R. Ewing			
	Mrs S. Burton	Woodbine			
	Mrs V. Cooper	Witham Golden Colonel			
Silver	Mrs S. Andrews	Winston II			
	Mr M. McLachlan	Rozanna Reign			
	Mrs P. Walkden	Jason II			
	Mrs R. Keogh	Rachel			
	Mrs M. Robinson	Maelor			
	Mrs D. Milnes	Calico Red of Oaklea			
	Mrs P. Merrington	Andy Pandy			
	Miss V. Parker	Woodbeer Charmian			
	Mrs M. Haes	Britannia			
	Miss R. Baillie	Jolly Dolly			
	Mrs F. Buchanan	Rajah			
	Mrs V. Akerman	Silver Dollar			
Bronze	Mrs J. Goodrich	Wide Boy Ben			
	Mr O. Hare	Brixmis Johnsal			
	Mrs J. Welcher	Kandy Bullard			

1982 (75 miles – 129km)

Gold	Mrs L. Beaney	Magnus	14.1hh	S	12
	Mr W. Francis	Boston Bay	15.3hh	G	9
	Mrs D. Boots	Hollington Dancing Flame	14.3hh	M	12
	Mrs G. Shutt	Triella	15.1hh	M	9
	Mrs P. Holloway	Clementine	15hh	M	15
	Mrs M. Townley	Miss Muffet	14.2hh	M	12
	Mrs M. Robinson	Maelor	15hh	M	13
	Mrs C. Hake	Merry Pepper Knox	14.3hh	G	8
	Mrs L. Jackson	Setra	15hh	M	12
	Mrs M. Windard	Canada Dry	16hh	G	8
	Mrs K. Bywater	Glanyrafon Rosita	15.2hh	M	11
Silver	Mrs J. Welcher	Kandy Bullard	15.3hh	M	8
	Miss J. Brewer	El Cid Sahran	15.1hh	G	13
	Mrs J. Martin	Swansong of Shamala	15.2hh	G	13
	Mrs P. Merrington	Andy Pandy	15.1hh	G	10
	Mrs L. Haes	Britannia	14.1hh	M	7
	Mrs C. Kennedy	Showgirl II	16hh	M	6
	Miss S. James	Demerara	14.1hh	G	7
	Mrs M. Burton	Byron	15.1hh	G	6
	Miss J. Reeve	Siouxtika Rey	15.2hh	M	7
	Miss G. Barber	Kirsty	15hh	M	8
	Miss A. Baggaley	Maxwell	15.1hh	G	10
	Miss S. Varnals	Smokey	14.3hh	G	15
	Mrs A. Toogood	Millstream Lady	15.1hh	M	8

	Mrs W. Oakins	Firelight Dancer	14.2hh	M	7

1983 (75 miles – 129km)

Gold	Mrs G. Shutt	Triella	15.2hh	M	10
	Mr C. Ware	Shaaban	15.3hh	G	10
	Mrs P. Holloway	Clementine	15hh	M	16
	Miss A. Kennedy	Showgirl II	16hh	M	7
Silver	Mrs L. Jackson	Setra	15hh	M	14
	Mrs S. Townley	Miss Muffet	14.2hh	M	13
	Miss V. Armstrong	Nickleby	15.3hh	G	8
	Miss E. Finney	Cleo	15.1hh	M	10
	Mrs D. Boots	Hollington Dancing Flame	14.2hh	M	13
	Mrs M. Burton	Byron	15.1hh	G	13
	Mrs V. Cooper	Witham Golden Colonel	15.1hh	G	10
Bronze	Mrs B. Johns	Benjamin	15.2hh	G	11
	Mrs S. Hill	Demerara	14.1hh	G	7
	Mrs Y. Tyson	Pandora	15hh	M	11
	Mrs J. Martin	Swansong of Shamala	15.2hh	G	7
	Mr S. Gennings	Solitaire	15hh	M	7
	Mrs N. Oliver	Princess Siona	15.1hh	M	9
	Mrs J. Brewer	El Cid Sahran	15.1hh	G	14
	Mrs P. Walkden	Jason II	14.2hh	G	9

1984 (75 miles – 129km)

Gold	Mrs S. Townley	Miss Muffet	14.2hh	M	14
	Mrs L. Finney	Cleo	15.1hh	M	11
	Mrs S. Scorey	Squire Tebeldi	14.3hh	G	10
	Mr A. Hayward	Richlings Bally Blaze	16.1hh	G	9
	Mr R. Heeley	Sabre III	15.3hh	G	9
	Mrs S. Bostlemann	Clara	15hh	M	11
	Mrs M. Butler	My Crispin	15.1hh	G	10
	Mrs M. Kelling	Spinway Wild Rose	14.1hh	M	10
	Mrs C. Hake	Crackerjack II	15.2hh	G	10
	Mrs J. Beaumont	R. Mellow Kinsman	15hh	S	7
	Mrs V. Cooper	Witham Golden Colonel	15.1hh	G	11
	Mr C Ware	Shaaban	15.3hh	G	11
	Miss D. Toomer-Baker	Nimrodel	16hh	M	10
	Mrs J. Wrinch	U.C. Foxglove	14.3hh	M	7
	Miss A. Kennedy	Showgirl II	16hh	M	8
	Mrs G. Shutt	Triella	15.2hh	M	11
	Mrs L. Dunn	Bonanza	15hh	S	8
	Mrs D. Boots	Hollington Dancing Flame	14.2hh	M	14
	Mrs P. James	Forest Fox	15.2hh	M	8
	Mrs A. Kellie	Autumn	15.2hh	M	8
	Mrs F. Ogilvy	Poste Haste	15.1hh	M	11
Silver	Mrs J. Jackson	Mulgrave Storm	16hh	M	10
	Miss H. Blair	Moondust	15hh	G	14
	Miss J. Reeve	Siouxtika Rey	15hh	M	9
	Mrs M. Whiting	Boyen No Ruz	14.3hh	G	8
	Mrs B. Johns	Benjamin	15.2hh	G	12
	Mrs J. Welcher	Victoria	15.1hh	M	19
	Mr W. Francis	Boston Bay	15.3hh	G	10
	Mrs S. Oakes	Yen	14hh	M	7
	Miss C. Long	Ginger II	14.2hh	M	9

	Mrs E. Kallaway	Flair of Glenbuckie	14hh	M	12
Bronze	Miss J. Timms	Jesta	15hh	G	13
	Mrs C. Lewis	Autumn Melody	14.3hh	M	11
	Mrs B. Jackson	Rattle On	15.1hh	M	14
	Miss H. Coaley	Red May	15.3hh	G	9
	Mrs P. Sommerwill	Gwenfo Mair	15hh	M	9

1985 (75 miles – 129km)

Gold	Miss A. Kennedy	Showgirl II	16hh	M	9
	Mrs U. Hutchinson	Skarry of Springfield	15hh	G	9
	Mr R. Heeley	Sabre II	15.3hh	G	10
	Mr D. Abercombie	Balou	16hh	G	9
	Mrs D. Passant	Ferhanoush	15.1hh	M	11
	Mrs A. Chapman	Dark Flight	15hh	G	7
	Mrs P. James	Forest Fox	15.2hh	M	9
	Mrs C. Tuggey	El Askar	14.3hh	G	10
	Mrs B. Bond	Fleur	14.2hh	M	7
	Mrs S. Derby	Caigers Picolo Roma	15.1hh	M	6
	Mrs J. Jackson	Mulgrave Storm	16hh	M	11
	Miss K. Townley	Miss Muffet	14.2hh	M	15
	Miss H. Blair	Moondust	15.2hh	G	15
	Miss J. Reeve	Siouxtika Rey	15.1hh	M	10
	Mr A. Hayward	Richlings Bally Blaze	16.1hh	G	10
	Miss J. Edwards	April Queen	15.2hh	M	10
	Miss A. Baggaley	Roseland Desert Song	15hh	G	9
	Miss L. Farrell	Tammy's Lad	15.1hh	G	7
	Mrs J. Klein	April Queen	15.2hh	M	10
	Mrs J. McGuinness	Chadwyke Goodness Gracious Me	15.2hh	G	7
	Mrs J. Wrinch	U.C. Foxglove	14.3hh	M	7
	Mrs D Scott	Newholme Sebastian	15.2hh	G	8
	Mrs J. Watts	Chadwyke Kazak	15hh	M	9
	Mrs G. Shutt	Triella	15.1hh	M	12
	Mrs L. Spencer-Allum	Pacific Glory	15.2hh	G	12
	Mrs R. Van Laun	Campions	14.3hh	G	12
	Mrs F. Ogilvy	Poste Haste	15.1hh	M	12
	Mrs A. Kent	Bintumani	15hh	M	8
	Mrs B. Wigley	Shushumi	15.1hh	M	13
	Mrs A. Ware	Sunlea Karanina	15hh	M	9
	Mrs J. Spencer	Bingham's Bullfinch	14.2hh	G	7
	Miss J. Lewis	Autumn Melody	14.3hh	M	11
	Mrs J. Welcher	Kandy Bullard	15.3hh	M	13
	Miss E. Carradine	Solfried	13.3hh	G	10
Silver	Mrs J. Maddock	Sueh	15.3hh	G	8
	Mrs S. Rowe	Pal-O-Mine	15hh	G	13
	Mrs H. Hilder	Star Queen	14.3hh	M	7
	Mrs V. Cooper	Witham Golden Colonel	15.1hh	G	12
	Mrs R. Alder	Lady Luck	14.2hh	M	9
	Miss J. Timms	Jesta	15hh	G	14
Bronze	Mrs M. Miller	San Miguel	16hh	G	9
	Mrs S. Dale	Golden Rhapsody	16hh	M	12
	Lt Cdr T. Hutchinson	Proper Charlie	16hh	G	12
	Mrs J. Francis	Rosador	16.3hh	M	10
	Miss J. Thorn	My Lovely	15.3hh	M	13

1986 (100 miles – 160km)
NO GOLD OR BRONZE AWARDS WERE WON THIS YEAR

Silver	Mrs M. Grove	Dubonnet	15.2hh	M	9
	Mrs P. James	Forest Fox	15.3hh	M	9
	Miss D. Toomer-Baker	Nimrodel	16hh	M	12
	Mrs D. Passant	Ferhanoush	15.1hh	M	12
Rosette	Mrs J. Taylor	Beltane Phoenix	15.2hh	G	7
	Mrs Y. Tyson	Caligular	15.2hh	G	7

1987 (100 miles – 160km)

Gold	Mrs J. Thomas	Egyptian Khalifa	15.3hh	G	7
	Mrs M. Grove	Dubonnet	15.2hh	M	10
	Mrs M. Ayton	Clouded Sky	–	–	–
	Miss V. Long	Tarim	15.2hh	S	11
	Mrs M. Barrett	Baccarat	14.2hh	M	16
	Mrs L. Finney	Showgirl II	16hh	M	12
Silver	Mrs D. Passant	Seagull	15.1hh	G	9
	Mrs J. Heeley	Dardanus	14.3hh	G	9
	Mrs M. Burton	Silver Lynx	15.2hh	G	8
	Mrs K. Trigg	Brookhouse Maestro	14.1hh	G	10
	Mrs Y. Tyson	Caligular	15.1hh	G	7
	Miss E. Carradine	Jigsaw Puzzle	16hh	M	10
	Miss L. Campbell	Sundance Boy	14.2hh	G	9
Bronze	Mrs L. Spencer-Allum	Pacific Glory	15.2hh	G	14
	Mr A. Fox-Carter	Peniarth Playboy	–	–	–
	Mrs A. Newton	Daoud Ibn Ahmoun	14.3hh	G	8
	Mrs J. Maddock	Sueh	15.3hh	G	10
	Mrs J. Allen	Pondicherry	14.2hh	M	11
	Mrs M. Eld	Gemma II	16.1hh	M	10
	Mr R. Heeley	Sabre III	15.3hh	G	13
	Mr J. Brooker	Lady Amblya	14.2hh	M	10

1988 (100 miles – 160km)
NO GOLD MEDALS WERE WON THIS YEAR

Silver	Mrs L. Finney	Showgirl II	16hh	M	12
Bronze	Mrs J. Petherick	Lucinda	15.3hh	M	7
	Mrs V. Cooper	Legend Alcoran	15hh	G	9
	Mrs A. McLean Foreman	Rattle On	15.1hh	G	18
	Miss L. Campbell	Witham Golden Colonel	15.1hh	G	15
	Mrs J. Thomas	Egyptian Khalifa	15.3hh	G	8
	Mrs Y. Tyson	Caligular	15.1hh	G	8
100 mile completion rosette	Mrs C. Cameron	White Trooper	15.1hh	G	9

2: DISTANCE & TIMES

Miles			Speed		
	6mph	*7mph*	*8mph*	*9mph*	*10mph*
10	1hr 40m	1hr 26m	1hr 15m	1hr 06m	1hr 00m
15	2hr 30m	2hr 09m	1hr 52m	1hr 40m	1hr 30m
20	3hr 20m	2hr 51m	2hr 30m	2hr 13m	2hr 00m
25	4hr 10m	3hr 34m	3hr 08m	2hr 47m	2hr 30m
30	5hr 00m	4hr 18m	4hr 44m	3hr 20m	3hr 00m
40	6hr 40m	5hr 42m	5hr 00m	4hr 16m	4hr 00m
50	8hr 20m	7hr 08m	6hr 16m	5hr 34m	5hr 00m

Time is calculated to the nearest minute

Metric Conversion

Miles	Kilometres		Miles	Kilometres
1	1.61		30	48.27
5	8.05		35	56.32
10	16.09		40	64.36
15	24.14		50	80.45
20	32.18		70	112.63
25	40.23		100	160.90

3: RECOMMENDED READING

The British Horse Society's *Notes on Long Distance Riding* (1979)
Drummond, Marcy. *Long Distance Riding* (Crowood Press, 1987)
Foster, Carol. *The Athletic Horse – His Selection, Work and Management* (Crowood Press, 1986)
Kydd, Rachel. *Long Distance Riding Explained* (Concorde Books, 1979)
Larter, Chris and Jackson, Tony. *Transporting your Horse or Pony* (David & Charles, 1987)
Meade, Richard. *Fit for Riding* (Batsford, 1984)
Pilliner, Sarah. *Getting Horses Fit* (Collins, 1986)
Rose, Mary. *The Horsemaster's Notebook* (Harrap, 1975)
Snow, Dr D.H. and Vogel, Colin. *Equine Fitness* (David & Charles, 1986)

4: USEFUL ADDRESSES

The Endurance Horse & Pony Society
of Great Britain
Paula Hancox
(secretary – introduction enquiries)
15 Newport Drive
Alcester
Warwickshire

Ossie Hare (membership enquiries)
Mill House
Mill Lane
Stoke Bruerne
Towcester
Northants NN12 7SH

The British Horse Society Long
   Distance Riding Group
Maggie Morton (secretary)
British Equestrian Centre
Stoneleigh
Kenilworth
Warwickshire CV8 2LR

Arab Horse Society
Goddards Green
Cranbrook
Kent TN17 3LP

Byways and Bridleways Trust
9 Queen Anne's Gate
London SW1H 9BY

Distance Rider Magazine
May Garland Farm
Chiddingly Road
Nr Heathfield
East Sussex TN21 0JJ

East Anglian Trail Riders Association
Jenny Kay (secretary)
Toad Hall
Low Common
Deopham
Wymondham
Norwich NR18 9DZ

Farrier's Registration Council
PO Box 49
East of England Showground
Peterborough PE2 0GU

Forestry Commission
231 Corstorphine Road
Edinburgh EG12 7AT

Highland Long Distance Riding Club
Candy Cameron
Drummond
Dores
Inverness
Scotland

Long Distance Riding Centre
Joan Davies
Fosse Way
Bourton-on-the-Water
Gloucestershire GL54 2DX

Society of Master Saddlers
H.C. Knight (Chief Executive)
The Cottage
4 Chapel Place
Bovey Tracey
Devon TQ13 9JA

The Welsh Long Distance Riding
   Centre
Jan Lloyd Rogers
Pine Lodge Stables
Rhydagaeau
Carmarthen
Wales

American Endurance Ride Conference
Toni King (Executive Director)
Suite 216
701 High Street
Auburn
CA 95603 USA

Australian Endurance Riding
   Association
Pauline Harris
PO Box 235
Gawler
South Australia

European Long Distance Rides
   Conference
Dr Riedler
Sonnenterrasse
CH-6030 Ebikon
Switzerland

North American Trail Ride Conference
Gloria Becker (secretary)
PO Box 20315
El Cajon

Index

Page numbers in *italics* indicate illustrations